THE FATEFUL TURN

From Individual Liberty to Collectivism

1880-1960

by

CLARENCE B. CARSON

The Foundation for Economic Education, Inc.

Irvington-on-Hudson, New York   1963

Author and Publisher

CLARENCE B. CARSON is a native of Alabama. He is a graduate of Auburn University and holds the Ph.D. from Vanderbilt University, his field of specialization being American social and intellectual history. He is a member of the American Studies Association. A lecturer of note in his chosen field, Dr. Carson is a frequent contributor to *The Freeman* and has had articles in other journals including *Modern Age,* the *Texas Quarterly,* the *Colorado Quarterly,* and *Spiritual Life.* He is currently Professor of American History at Grove City College in Pennsylvania.

~ ~ ~

THE FOUNDATION FOR ECONOMIC EDUCATION is an educational champion of private ownership, the free market, the profit and loss system, and limited government. It is nonprofit and nonpolitical. Sample copies of the Foundation's monthly journal, *The Freeman,* as well as a list of books and other publications, are available on request.

Published April, 1963

IN MEMORIAM

to

Donald Carson

Acknowledgments

The following articles, reprinted here in whole or in part, appeared in *The Freeman:*

"Individualism versus *Common*ism."
"The Foundations of American Liberty."
"Undermining the Foundations."
"Circumstances Hostile to Liberty."
"A Collectivist Curvature of the Mind."
"The Defamation of the American Tradition."
"The Road to Collectivism."
"Having Our Cake and Eating It, Too."
"Of Rights—Natural and Arbitrary."
"A Rebirth of Liberty."
" 'You Can't Turn Back the Clock.' "

"The Concept of Democracy and John Dewey" appeared in *Modern Age,* and is used by permission.

An excerpt appears from "New Words for Our Time," published in *The Colorado Quarterly,* and is used by permission.

Contents

Author's Preface

THIS BOOK lies somewhere between a historical monograph and a series of essays joined by a central theme. It combines, too, the results of historical research, broad historical interpretation, and personal observation. Sometimes I have focused upon very particular events and men, while at others I have offered broad generalizations. It is unlikely that anyone would be an authority upon all the matters I have touched upon, and certainly I am not. But the truth of what I have to say does not depend upon me as an authority, but upon the accuracy of the facts adduced, the validity of the generalizations offered, and the truth which undergirds my viewpoints.

This is an attempt to explain what has happened to the beliefs and practices supporting individual liberty in America in the last eighty years or so. About this, I have a thesis and a viewpoint. My thesis is that the beliefs which supported individual liberty have been undermined by thinkers, that this undermining prepared the way for and has been accompanied by the spreading of collectivist ideas, and that in the twentieth century collectivism has increasingly come to inform our practices and institutions.

I have a viewpoint, too. I believe in individual liberty.

I believe that the recognition of it and the protection of it is the greatest social concern, along with a just order within which it can subsist. I believe that individual liberty is not only of temporal but also of ultimate importance. If such beliefs—"biases"?—disqualify me from writing history, then so be it. I know of no reason why such beliefs should require the suppression of facts or the telling of less than the truth, though, of course, I don't know the whole of it.

The first two chapters are introductory in character. The first chapter provides an overview of the remainder of the book and a characterization of the contest among ideas that has been going on for the past eighty years. The second chapter provides the vantage point in the American tradition of liberty from which the developments are viewed. Chapters 3 through 7 are an attempt to describe the thrust to collectivism, sometimes broadly and at others more specifically: the development and propagation of an ideology, the formation of movements, the men and ideas, and the beginning of the political realization of collectivist ideas. Chapters 8 and 9 deal with some of the efforts to defend individualism and their failure. Chapter 10 attempts to describe collectivism being made into an orthodoxy after World War II. The remaining chapters are by way of being critiques of the collectivist assumptions and some thoughts about the possibility of turning the tide of collectivism, not so much history as the reflections of a student of history.

I have a debt of gratitude to pay to those who have given me assistance and encouragement over the years. I began to get the first inklings of this thesis while doing my Master's thesis at what is now Auburn University. The study was of Herbert Hoover and his concept of the role of government. Some of the evidence which is presented in chapter 9 is gleaned from that study. I should like especially to thank Professor Robert L. Parton for his help in the preparation of that thesis. Many of the ideas presented here began to take definite shape during my work on my doctoral dissertation at Vanderbilt University. To Professor Henry L. Swint of that institution who has encouraged, stimulated, criticized, and directed some of my work, I am especially grateful. Let me hasten to add that neither of these gentlemen has seen the manuscript for this book, and that they bear no responsibility for such weaknesses as it may have.

The staff of The Foundation for Economic Education has given invaluable aid to me in the preparation of this book. More particularly has Dr. Paul L. Poirot served as editor, critic, soother of ruffled feelings, mediator in disputes, and bolsterer of ego in times of despondency. He has, to my knowledge, no equal in promptness and no superior in decisiveness. I am indebted, too, to Mrs. Eleanor Orsini for aid in correcting proofs and to Miss Vernelia Crawford for her work on the index. All of this is by way of a tribute to the good judgment and integrity of Mr. Leonard E. Read who has assembled these people at the Foundation.

I received financial assistance from the Southern Fellowship Fund while working on my dissertation from which some of these ideas stem and from the Pew Foundation for the publication of this book. However, none of these people or organizations are in any way responsible for any errors of fact, invalid generalizations, or departures from truth which may have occurred. That responsibility is mine alone. Nor should their assistance be construed as endorsement of particular ideas or interpretations.

My greatest debt of all is to my wife, Myrtice Sears Carson, who has borne graciously the morose silences which have preceded, accompanied, and followed my spurts of writing, who has read copy for errors and attempted to penetrate my prose, and who has taken pleasure in anything that resembled achievement.

CLARENCE B. CARSON
Grove City, Pennsylvania
December 1962

1. (PROLOGUE)

Individualism versus *Commonism*

THERE IS NO difficulty today in getting assent to the proposition that something untoward has happened to individualism in America. It is a commonplace saying that conformity has been raised to the position of a prime virtue and that the individual is being sacrificed to the group. There has been a spate of books since World War II devoted to expounding this thesis. William H. Whyte, in *The Organization Man*, contends that even the most powerful spokesman of individualism, the corporation man, is using the language of individualism to "stave off the thought that he himself is in a collective as pervading as any ever dreamed of by the reformers, the intellectuals, and the utopian visionaries he so regularly warns against."[1] David Riesman and colleagues, in *The Lonely Crowd*, detail the loss of independence by Americans and ascribe it to a change in the American character from "inner direction" to "other direction." Erich Kahler, in a recent work, declares: "Today we are witnessing and are deeply involved in a huge process of human transformation. This transformation seems to tend toward some formation beyond the individual. However, it

---

[1] William H. Whyte, Jr., *The Organization Man* (Garden City, N.Y.: George Braziller, Inc., 1957), p. 6.

manifests itself in diverse processes of disruption or in-
validation of the individual."[2]

The literature proclaiming the existence and analyzing the phenomena of conformity is bountiful. It runs
the gamut from novels to popular treatises to psychological explorations to sociological monographs, from
The Man in the Gray Flannel Suit to *The Exurbanites* to
The Hidden Persuaders to *A Nation of Sheep*. Reports
come in that college students are passive, that young
men seek secure positions in giant corporations, that
home buyers seek domicile in suburbia with its row
upon row of uniform houses, that men prefer public
relief to migration in search of new jobs.

The ease of manipulating Americans *en masse* is apparent to any perceptive observer. For several decades
now Americans have been prone to mass crazes from
Mah Jong to hula hoops, to hero worship from Charles
A. Lindbergh to Elvis Presley, to popular songs, to mati-
nee idols, and to all sorts of fads. National propaganda
has apparently been able, in the last twenty years, to
get us to hate the Germans and Italians, despise the
Russians, love the Finns, loathe the Japanese, embrace
the Russians, ignore the Finns, admire the Germans,
Italians, and Japanese, and suspect the Russians, in that
order.

As I said, there is much agreement that individualism
has declined precipitately in America. But at this point
consensus ends sharply. There must be almost as many
explanations of the phenomena as there are accounts
of it. Some will offer such standard explanations as in-

---

[2] Erich Kahler, *The Tower and the Abyss* (New York:
George Braziller, Inc., 1957), p. xiii.

dustrialization, urbanization, the end of the frontier, and the population increase. Others attach the change to such developments as advertising, propaganda, the mass media of communication, the progressive methods of education, the growth of the corporation, the spread of unionism, the enactment of near universal suffrage, or the strained international situation. As usual, we strain at gnats and swallow camels. The above developments doubtless have had a debilitating effect upon the practice of individualism in America. But whether they are taken separately or considered in concert, they are symptoms of the ailment, not the efficient cause. They are the *means* by which individualism has been overturned, not the *end* which has wrought the change.

The main reason why we have not recognized the sources of the change from individualism in America is that they have not been defined in terms of individualism. Many of those who have worked to undermine the premises of individualism and to institute non-individualistic practices have done so in the name of the individual. They have been able to do this because, in part, they were the proponents of and were able to operate within a context of relativism, irrationalism, and disemboweled romanticism. They could use vague language and did not find it necessary to define their ends clearly. In consequence, they have been able to hack away most of the framework of individualism with only a minimum of coherent objections from the defenders of it.

The task which I propose to undertake here is to define both individualism and that which has undermined it in such a way that they can be identified. This is only a first step toward understanding what has happened to individualism historically, but it is a necessary step. The definitions will both be abstracted from the actual historical development of the ideas in America.

Individualism Defined

Individualism, as an idea or set of beliefs, is the belief in the *primary* and *final* importance of the individual. That is, it is the belief that the individual is the prime unit out of which arise all other units, whether they be groups, collectives, organizations, societies, states, or civilizations. Individualists usually hold that since these groupings were brought into being by combinations of individuals, they exist for the individual. The individual is the final unit in that it is his fulfillment for which the combinations exist. Eschatologically, the individual is the ultimate unit, in that he alone, not any group, survives eternally. But final unit may be a better phrase because there have been individualists both among temporally oriented humanists and among those who believe in life beyond this earth.

Modern (post-Medieval) thought about individualism has focused upon the uniqueness of each individual. It is a major tenet of individualism that it is the differences, the uniqueness, from one man to another which constitute the real significance of the individual. It is a man's peculiar talents, needs, interests, purposes, and possessions which differentiate him from other men and make him so important. All that he holds in common with other men can serve only to meld him into an undifferentiated mass. His distinct being, his creativity, his significant existence, derive and proceed from his uniqueness.

Room for the development of the uniqueness of the individual is the major social requirement of individualism. Many of the ideas associated with individualism derive from this need. Freedom, for example, is a *sine qua non* of individualism just as coercion is anathema to it. The individual must be free to determine his purposes, free to seek to fulfill his needs, free to associate or not to associate with others in pursuing his goals.

It does not follow that the way must be paved for him, or that he will achieve his fulfillment if he is solicitously aided by others. Rather, the individual needs a society in which he is put on his own to provide for his needs, in which he is at liberty to pursue his goals, in which when he has developed his potentiality it stands a chance of being rewarded, in which relations are voluntary, in which pressures and forces are kept at a minimum. Such, at any rate, was the freedom which nineteenth century individualists thought was pertinent to their development.

Such freedom would make society difficult if there were not a corresponding development of individual *responsibility*. Individualism *was* a *social* theory, and many exponents of it made individual responsibility a major requirement for its embodiment in society. Logically, if the individual is free to develop his potentialities, he is responsible for the consequences of their development or for his activities as he develops.

Another corollary was that each individual's freedom ends where another's begins. When such a principle was applied to property rights, it meant that the law which protected one man's property from trespass restrained him from trespassing on the property of another. Ideally, it would be better if the individual had developed a strong sense of responsibility for his actions. Failing this, however, society was once thought to be serving a salutary function when it held an individual responsible when he violated the rights of other individuals. It would be in keeping with individualism to punish a man for intrusion upon the sphere of another. On the other hand, to remove the opportunity for such intrusion would not be individualistic; it would result, most likely, in a curtailment of liberty.

Individualism, liberty, and responsibility were all premised upon the philosophical foundation of a belief in the *freedom of the will*, in the belief that it is possible to make free choices. It is anachronistic to hold an individual responsible for behavior which he did not initiate. To state the principle positively, it is axiomatic that the orginator of an action is responsible for its consequences. Logical consistency demands that if an individual is to be held responsible for an action he must have initiated it either by choice, by a derelict failure to choose, or, at least, that choice in that instance was possible. Once admit the rule of necessity or determinism and the foundation of individual responsibility would be removed and the counterbalance to freedom have been destroyed.

Less obviously, the belief in individualism, as the idea developed in the nineteenth century, was founded directly upon the role that choice was supposed to play in the development of a man. According to this interpretation, the uniqueness of the individual resulted from day to day choices which led either to the realization of the individual or to his disintegration. Hence, the final or ultimate condition of the individual depended upon his choices.

Once free choice ceases to be the primary factor in men's assessment of a man's position or actions, it will become increasingly difficult to defend practical liberty. If choice has not played a primary role in producing the inequities among men, for example, it will be hard to reconcile these inequities with our sense of justice. Those who have less are deprived not because of their failure but by the scheme of things. In addition, if men act out of necessity, liberty has no ultimate significance; it serves mainly to keep some portion of the population out of prison, for men cannot act otherwise than they do. Such liberty as a society permitted would probably be based upon calculations about the desires of men and the practicality of restraining some of them by removing the opportunity for their fulfillment. In short, liberty would be reduced to permission to do whatever it would be possible to do.

To sum up, the major tenets of individualism are: belief in the primary and final importance of the individual, emphasis upon that which is unique in each man, insistence upon liberty for the realization of the individual, individual responsibility, and freedom of the will. These form the bedrock of ideas which are essential to individualism. They have been supported in the modern era by such divergent ideas as nominalism, Arminianism, rationalism, voluntarism, and idealism. The ideas associated with individualism have been articu-

lated in American (and to some extent in European) society in such institutions and practices as constitutional
government, establishment of a private sphere by re-
stricting governmental actions by a Bill of Rights, private property, removal of social rules governing inherit-
ance (abolition of primogeniture and entail), free trade,
voluntary church membership, individual choice of marriage partners, private or voluntary associations for providing charity, and so forth.

Undermined by Commonism

Individualism has been losing its sway over Americans in the last seventy or eighty years, sometimes
gradually, sometimes dramatically and swiftly. This loss
is manifested in as simple a matter as the necessity
which men now feel to begin any undertaking, regardless of its character or complexity, by forming a committee, establishing a foundation or institute, charter-
ing a corporation, or organizing a club or movement.
It is apparent in the massive shifts to governmental responsibility and the proliferation of legalistic rules and
regulations which govern our lives. It is evinced in the
curtailment of the individual's control of his affairs
(compulsory health insurance required by employers and
social security by government), in the loss of parental
responsibility for and control over children, in governmental propaganda and examination of beliefs.

Circumstances have, of course, set the stage for this
shift away from individualism, but they have not determined its direction nor guided us into the new course
we have set for ourselves. That role has been played by

men and ideas, or men under the sway of ideas. There has been a definite direction and it was established on the basis of some fairly definite ideas. The trouble we have had in recognizing them has been the variety of names by which the proponents of these changes have been called and the different means they have proposed toward a common end which they have not been too forward in naming. These men have been supplanting individualism and implanting a new ethos in America. There are several words in current usage which do service as opposites of individualism, i.e., collectivism, socialism, communism, and, I suspect, democracy, though some would heatedly debate the inclusion of the latter. Lester Frank Ward suggested sociocracy, but it did not catch on. The words in common usage are either too vague, too specialized, or too freighted with emotional content for descriptive use. I would like to use a coined word to describe the ethos which has been replacing individualism.

The word is *commoni*sm.

*Commoni*sm has the disadvantage of differing from communism by only one letter in its spelling, but it is apt, nonetheless, for descriptive purposes. It implies the end or purpose of this ethos, diametrically opposes it to individualism, and describes the methods by which the end is to be achieved. *Commoni*sm focuses attention upon the common needs, interests, and purposes of mankind, not upon the ways in which men differ from one another. Its main concern is with those things which men share with one another. For example, all men share certain appetites, such as those for food, for warmth, and for attention. The *commoni*st would organize society in such a way as to provide all of these efficiently to everyone.

*Common*ism is the belief that the individual derives his being from the commonality, and derives his *raison d'etre* from society. Implicitly, and sometimes explicitly, *common*ism is the view that the individual exists for society. The *common*ist is at ease among such terms and phrases as *mankind, general welfare, humanity,* the *people,* the *common good,* and the *brotherhood of man,* all of which he tends to interpret in light of the shared physical needs or desires of men. To the *common*ist it is likely to be the group, collective, state, society, or mankind which endures while the individual terminates with death. The individual has meaning only as he is a part of the group. Such rights and privileges as he possesses come to him from the group and are his during the sufferance of the group. The contemporary *common*ist does not usually recognize anything beyond the collective—mankind, humanity, common welfare—to which to appeal. When the people have spoken, the last word has been said.

The *common*ist may not be an absolute determinist, though he frequently is, but he does attach preponderant importance to heredity and environment in explaining human behavior and human differences. The terms in which he defines his view may differ—economic determinism, environmentalism, psychological determinism, but the belief that choice is unnecessary to account for human behavior is never far away. He accepts a common responsibility for everything that happens and proclaims the common responsibility of each of us for all of us.

The General Area of Conflict

Individualism versus *commonism*—these two terms represent poles between which the changes and conflicts of recent American history can be fruitfully viewed. They may not encompass all that has taken place, but they include enough to throw the developments during these years into revealing relief. They place the conflicts within Congress, the difficult decisions of Presidents, the tendency of court actions into a meaningful context. It is not stretching the point to say that the major legislative and legal contests of the last seventy years—the contests over antitrust acts, the creation of regulatory agencies, espionage and sedition acts, the mobilizations for wars, the means of fighting depression, the regulation of organized labor—have had overtones of the general conflict between individualism and *commonism*.

The battles between reformers and conservatives can be profitably viewed in the light of this conflict. Reformers have tended to want to institute *commonism* and conservatives have stood, more often than not, for the old individualistic way—whether the reformer be Theodore Roosevelt or the conservative be Robert A. Taft. Of course, the issue has not always been clear-cut; the alternatives have not always been spelled out; the choices have frequently been between means to the same end.

The successes of *commonism* can be measured in terms of the spread of unionism, the growth of trusts and corporations, the centralization of authority in Washington, the ubiquitous activities of bureaucracies, the proliferation of welfare programs, the assumption of public responsibility for everything from education to housing, the triumph of the "clear and present danger

doctrine" of the courts, the sanction of the curtailment
of liberties under the rubric of the police powers of the
state, and the general ease of legitimating any governmental activity which is claimed to be in the interest of
the general welfare. Individualists carried out successful holding actions when voluntarism was preserved,
when individual liberty was sustained, when private
property was preserved (though the attack has not been
directly against private property any more than it has
against individual liberty), when governmental action
was forestalled, when they succeeded in retaining any
responsibility and function for the individual.

*Common*ism began to take shape in the thinking and
writing of some American intellectuals in the latter part
of the nineteenth century. Its keynote can be found in a
book published by the sociologist, Lester Frank Ward, in
1893. He said:

> The individual has reigned long enough. The day
> has come for society to take its affairs into its own
> hands and shape its own destinies. The individual has
> acted as best he could. He has acted in the only way
> he could. With a consciousness, will, and intellect of
> his own he could do nothing else than pursue his nat-
> ural ends. He should not be denounced nor called any
> names. He should not even be blamed. Nay, he should
> be praised, and even *imitated*. Society should learn its
> great lesson from him, should follow the path he has
> so clearly laid out that leads to success. It should im-
> agine itself an individual, with all the interests of an
> individual, and becoming fully *conscious* of these
> interests it should pursue them with the same indomi-
> table will with which the individual pursues his in-
> terests. Not only this, it must be guided, as he is
> guided, by the social *intellect,* armed with all the

knowledge that all individuals combined, with so great labor, zeal, and talent have placed in its possession, constituting the social intelligence.[3]

The list of propagators and progenitors of *commonism* should include Henry George, Richard Ely, Henry Demarest Lloyd, Edward Bellamy, Daniel De Leon, Eugene Debs, Thorstein Veblen, and Jack London, among others. It was forwarded by socialists, communists, muckrakers, preachers of the Social Gospel, nationalists, educationists, and various and assorted Progressives. It was promoted by the development of a "social conscience" and instituted by people who styled themselves liberals.

Individualists were in a majority at the outset of the conflict, of course. At the beginning of the twentieth century they held positions of power and influence. They could denounce, cajole, laugh at, and perhaps persecute the proponents of *commonism*. Even so, the tide was turning the other way; many who talked the language of individualism were deeply embroiled in the business of protecting corporations, promoting imperialistic ventures, putting down unions by the national guard, and turning to government to solve problems. The hammer blows of twentieth century wars and depression blinded many to the nature of the conflict of ideas, and the *commonists* stood ready with their programs to take over.

We are still in the midst of the massive shift from individualism to *commonism* so far as institutions and practices are concerned. But the great change in ideas

---

[3] Lester F. Ward, "Sociocracy," *American Thought: Civil War to World War I*, intro. by Perry Miller (New York: Holt, Rinehart & Winston, Inc., 1957), pp. 113-14.

and beliefs which prepared the way for it took place—
so far as most of the populace was concerned—in the
first three or four decades of this century. *Common*ist
ideas became the common possession of Americans because they came to permeate the literature, the language, the sermons, the lectures, and the thought of
opinion makers.

There must have been many Americans who did not
fall under the sway of *common*ism. Undoubtedly, too,
there were untold millions who began to use and think
in terms of these ideas unwittingly, and who would have
been horrified to discover that any radical change had
taken place in their thinking. But these were without
effective leadership. The initiative in the contest slipped
from the individualists to the *common*ists in this century. Those who spoke for individualism became defenders and apologists of it, were themselves infected by the
new ideas and convinced that they must accept some
of the programs of the reformers. They compromised.
At most, they fought delaying actions, and, as politicians, became known as the "rear guard." Those who
think of what to do when some new problem or issue
arises stopped thinking of ways to deal with it by individual action and proposed some kind of collective action.

The New Orthodoxy

By the mid-twentieth century *common*istic ideas were
established in America, and they have been rapidly
hardening into an inflexible orthodoxy. It is this orthodoxy which prescribes that every problem must be

solved by group action, that world peace must be sought collectively, that the problems of education must be met by federal aid, that symphony orchestras bearing the names of various cities must be supported by money from the national government, that a secularized missionary effort under the auspices of the Peace Corps shall be financed by public (i.e., tax) money, that the exploration of space shall be undertaken by governments.

These various programs pass for new ideas when they are first brought forth in current intellectual circles. In fact, they are not that at all. They are rather the articulation of the notions implicit in the assumptions of *commonism*. Indeed, the penchant for raising all difficulties to the national level and defining them as national problems witnesses to a curvature of the mind hardened into an habitual path.

I compress too much, passing over the exceptions, modifications, and subtleties. But it was not my purpose in what I have said to relate the history of the last seventy years. My intention is to call attention to the outline of it to validate the view that the changes of these years can be brought into focus in such a way that their significance stands out by examining them between the poles of individualism versus *commonism*.

2.

The Foundations of American Liberty

THERE IS A growing awareness that we Americans, individually and as a people, have lost our bearings. Some try to still the uneasiness that this awareness arouses by adopting public postures of confidence. Others react by denouncing those who suggest that everything is not just as it should be. Groups are being formed throughout the land that focus on this or that ailment as the source of our troubles. The extremes are represented by the quietism of President Kennedy and the near hysteria of the Minute Men.

Our actual condition may be likened to that of a company of people which, having set out upon a journey, has been lost in a jungle. The acknowledged leaders, fearing to divide and frighten the people, refuse to admit they have lost their way. As for the rest, they are divided, and fall roughly into three camps. The first group would have everyone turn back, retracing their steps to the place from whence they had come. The second group favors staying where they are. The situation, they say, is tolerable, and conditions are familiar. The third group, to which the leaders profess to belong, urges moving on, though none claims to know where such a course would lead. Dangers lie behind, for many have seen them and some have fallen victim to them on the way. Ahead lie even more formidable dangers, possibly, and the way is not even marked out. There is considerable inducement for the company to stay where they are, and, despite the bold proclamations of the leaders about pressing on to new frontiers, a disinterested observer would be able to discern little movement, if the milling around be discounted.

This parable, however, does little more than reduce our conditions to a figurative language, in terms of which we may be able to grasp it. It affirms the estimate that we have lost our way. But why are we lost? What is it that we have lost? How is our sense of direction (or purpose) to be restored?

We have already taken some of the false paths out of the wilderness. There is no need, for example, to appoint commissions of men, whose sense of reality has been dulled by years of bureaucratic endeavor, to name national goals. They will, predictably and demonstrably (re: President's Commission on National Goals), only rework the tired clichés of a bankrupt "liberalism." Nor should we turn to the psychologizers who will give us their pet theories about why we *think* something is wrong. Already men of this ilk are spreading their preconceived explanations of the sources of the new conservatism. It would be wiser to follow medical practice and check the physical condition of the patient first before concluding that his ills are psychological. Nor, if we have lost our sense of purpose, as I think, should the contest with the Soviet Union for world influence be substituted for real and vital purposes. It is of little value to affirm that communism conflicts with our way of life if we do not know what that way is.

Unity that forever depends upon external threats of destruction is negative and pointless. If all enemies were to disappear, there would be every incentive to invent one, as George Orwell foresaw in *1984*. We have followed too long the path of mustering national action by proclaiming national emergencies. That Presidents should find it necessary to do this simply underscores the loss of direction, purpose, and orientation.

Mark well, too, that the cry for leaders and ideologies, which wells up from among us, is the preface to the creation of dictatorships and totalitarian states. Twentieth century Europe has already followed this broad path to destruction. Must we follow their example, our eyes closed to the already demonstrated catastrophe which awaits at its end?

Back to Basic Principles

There is another way whose outline has begun to take shape for some of us. Let me describe it first by way of analogy. A man who realizes that he may have lost his way will begin to look for familiar landmarks. If there are none ahead, he does well to turn back and to retrace his steps to the point where he knows he is on the right road. In terms of national purpose, this means a return to foundations. It means that the foundations will have to be uncovered and explored anew, and that plans for action will have to be measured in terms of consistency with them.

This is no easy way. There are no guarantees that it will work. No leaders can shoulder the burden while we bask in the sunshine of their favor. Yet it accords well with the basic experience of man, and this in itself should commend the course to us.

Indeed, our very terminology implies that retracing our steps is the right course. That we are lost suggests that once we were on the right path. The initial effort, then, should be made to rediscover the way, to return to the point where we went astray. In short, the problem is in part historical. That it should be so is a tremendous advantage. It means that we can utilize memory and imagination, appealing to such records as have been kept along the way. This part of the task is one for the historian, which is why I venture to speak.

Let us return first, not to the place where we went astray, but to the point from which we started. The historical course of America was plotted from that point of the compass of our ideals marked Liberty. Our disorientation can only mean that we have wandered, or been led, off this course. The writings of the Founding Fathers are replete with references to liberty as the goal. George Washington did not expect to be gainsaid when he said, in his Farewell Address, "Interwoven as is the love of liberty, with every ligament of your hearts, no recommendation of mine is necessary to fortify or confirm the attachment."

All of the major documents of our Revolutionary and early Constitutional era are premised on this attachment to liberty. Nor would anyone have thought it possible at that time to found a government which would preserve liberty if a time should come when Americans should cease to venerate it. Our quest for foundations, then, will begin and end with an exploration of the foundations of American liberty.

The three basic foundations of our liberty are: (1) beliefs which support it, (2) institutions which protect it, and (3) personal independence without which it is meaningless and impossible.

Beliefs Which Support Liberty

Let us turn first to the beliefs which support liberty. Liberty is *not* an end in and of itself. It is not even an ideal in the Platonic sense; that is, it does not rank with Truth, Beauty, Goodness, and Justice. Rather, liberty is a condition, a means to greater ends, not less but more important for that very reason. Choice is possible among many goals and the several ideals when there is liberty, but without liberty there is no choice. Liberty is the gateway through which choice is made possible; it is the keystone of the arch of individual fulfillment and social progress.

Those men who conceived and founded these United States must have known something of the deep underlying significance of liberty, but they rarely, if ever, expounded upon it. Much of the thought of the eighteenth century (that thought which informed our institutions and practices) was superficial, but it rested upon a profound legacy of traditions and beliefs. The Founding Fathers were men of affairs, not philosophers, and they did not customarily expose the deep roots of their beliefs. Indeed, they felt no need to do so, for they supposed their beliefs to be deeply rooted and secure.

We are not so happily situated in our times. For us it is necessary to learn again the deep meanings of things which, because they lay beneath the surface of things, have been forgotten. The reverence for liberty can only be reawakened by re-establishing its connection with a reality which gives it vitality.

Liberty was once believed to be a God-given condition. The respect for and observance of it had the force of divine imperative. Thinkers of the eighteenth century conceived the matter in this way. God created the universe and all the natural things that are in it. In so doing, He provided natural conditions of liberty, thus implicitly setting His seal upon liberty as the proper condition for man.

There are no restraints, only punishments, built into the natural scheme. Thus, man is at liberty to jump from a high cliff; but if he does so in violation of natural law, he will likely be punished with a broken neck. Man, in nature, is free, for the simple reason that he is not restrained. This is the liberty with which man is endowed by the "Nature and Nature's God" to which Jefferson refers in the Declaration of Independence.

Liberty, then, is a natural right based on a condition prior to man. Restraints are tyrannical efforts of man to meddle with the natural (divine) order. Tyranny is a violation of ultimate law; to acquiesce in it is tacitly to participate in the abrogation of divine law.

Quite properly, the Founding Fathers did *not* spell out the specific ends for which liberty exists. They did set forth in the Preamble to the Constitution the purposes for founding a government, but they did not presume to announce the purpose of life for individuals within it or the goals of the society itself. Had they done so, they would have been setting the stage for some new tyranny which could bend men toward that end. Governments

can act only by coercion, whether it be the coercion of
the mind by propaganda or the coercion of the body by
force. When government acts to realize an ideology—
any ideology—it must become totalitarian. It is one
thing to have a system of ideas (an ideology, if that
hateful word must be used); it is quite another to pre-
scribe that system of ideas for everyone in the society
by law.

There is a vast difference between the Declaration of
Independence and the United States Constitution. The
Declaration has an explicit ideology while the Constitution has none. The first is a revolutionary document,
drawn and used primarily for purposes of propaganda.
The second is a carefully drawn instrument to provide
for the governance of a people. The Declaration is not
now, never was, and never should become a part of the
law of this land. Everyone should be free to accept its
basic premises, as I do, but no one should be compelled
to believe anything. The men who founded this country believed that free men should be entrusted with the
task of providing for their needs, defining their purposes, and devising means to their ends.

Many, perhaps most, Americans in the eighteenth and
nineteenth centuries believed that the ultimate aim of
life is the eternal salvation of the soul. These United
States were founded on the premise that salvation is
primarily an individual rather than a social matter. It
is individual in that only individual souls survive in
eternity, not groups, nor collectives, nor states. It is a
spiritual condition, and lies beyond the power of the
state to grant, withhold, compel, or require. The most
that the state can do is to acknowledge that liberty

within which each man may use his varied talents, make his own momentous choices, give voice to his particular insights into truth, obey those divine imperatives which fall to his lot, and develop such potentialities as are latent within him.

So far as earthly social goals were concerned, our political progenitors believed implicitly that the general welfare would be advanced in conditions of greatest liberty for all. If it were not, each individual would have himself primarily to blame. The term general welfare has now been subverted to the ends of welfare statists who have given it the utilitarian connotation of the greatest good for the greatest number. Yet it would have been inconsistent with the government which they actually created if the Founders had used general welfare in this sense in either the Preamble or elsewhere in the Constitution.

The greatest good for the greatest number envisions government action for interest groups. Yet it is likely that general welfare was conceived individually, not collectively, by most men who sat in the Constitutional Convention. And it is possible to conceive of action for the general welfare that is in the interest of each and every individual. For example, it is in the interest of everyone that a murderer be apprehended and restrained. In the interest of the murderer, too? Yes, for if he cannot control himself, he needs to be controlled by others. If he can but will not control himself, *he* needs to be punished. It is the character of a right action that it is good for those disadvantaged as well as those advantaged by it. It is in the nature of things, too, that if a government is to act only in the interest of everyone,

it will be limited in those actions it can take. This is precisely the position of the Founding Fathers.

Liberty was conceived to be not only individually but
also socially beneficent. Social progress is never the justification of liberty (a false trail which some thinkers
have taken), but it can be and is a valuable by-product.
Free men will rise or fall on their own merits, prosper or
fail as they exert themselves, and give or take as they
have wisely used their resources. Free men pay a price
for their freedom. They are responsible for their own
well-being.

Freedom and Responsibility

This is true because freedom and responsibility are
opposite sides of the same coin. Diminish one by a whit
and you reduce the other in the same measure. Thus,
when men are free, there are powerful incentives to
build, create, and invent things that they can sell to or
exchange with other men. Progress, then, is an almost
inevitable result of leaving men to their own devices in
attracting consumers for their products and thus providing for their own needs.

Liberty is intellectually unsupportable without certain
other beliefs. It is premised on freedom of the mind and
will. Freedom of the mind means that the mind can
reason out conclusions, can uncompulsively examine
evidence, can choose among ideas the one that is truest
or best supported by evidence. Freedom of the will
means the possibility of making uncompelled choices
and translating these into corresponding actions.

If man is not free in these senses, he is not responsible for his actions. If he is not responsible for his actions, liberty is an unconscionable burden to impose upon man and an unworkable arrangement for society. Liberty is practicable only if men can be held accountable for the harm that they do to others. Otherwise, they would have to be constrained from committing their acts, which would mean in effect that there could be no liberty. Moreover, if men are not *primarily* responsible for their conditions, then inequalities cannot be squared with our fundamental sense of justice.

Our forefathers had yet another belief which mightily buttressed individual liberty. They believed that man is distinctly a rational being, that he is capable of subordinating his passions to logic and submitting to it as arbiter. Reason was believed to be both the means by which man came to an understanding of his world and the primary protection individuals have against the aggression of others upon their rights. The individual is powerless against combinations of men if might rules in the world.

But our ancestors believed that reason, not might, should hold sway in the common affairs of men. As Jefferson put it in his First Inaugural Address, "All, too, will bear in mind this sacred principle, that though the will of the majority is in all cases to prevail, that will to be rightful must be reasonable. . . ." Reason, if men will submit to it, is a lever by which the individual can move groups and states to observe his rights and yield to something beyond either one or many. For note that reason is higher authority, man-possessed but not man-made. Our Republic was contrived in this world, but its foundations lay in one beyond.

The above, then, are the intellectual foundations of American liberty: natural law, freedom of the mind and will, individual responsibility, and rationalism. These in turn were given evocative power by the belief that there is a God who imbedded his immutable laws in the visible universe, that the individual has a worth not measurable in human terms, that each individual's good is inseparable from the general welfare, and that liberty is priceless for the individual and socially beneficial.

Institutions Which Protect Liberty

The institutional protections of our liberties were laid down in the early years of the Republic. The individual was protected from his government by enumerations of powers granted and prohibitions aimed at preventing governments from exercising certain forbidden powers. The agents of the government were limited in their exercise of power by the separation of powers.

The populace at large was inhibited from taking precipitate actions by the representative principle and by the differing terms of office of those elected. The populace was further limited by making the judiciary—the final protectors of individual liberty—appointive rather than elective. The federal system of government—a system in which powers are divided between the central and local governments—was conceived as a further protection of liberty.

Many of the protections of individual liberty were not new to the United States; they were preserved and continued. Such were the right to a writ of habeas corpus, the requirement that a man be deprived of his life or liberty only by due process of law, and the right to own and use property. New protections were set forth as well, however: the constitutional prohibitions against bills of attainder and ex post facto laws, the state disestablishment of churches, the abolition of primogeniture and entail.

Personal independence was forwarded by American conditions and practices. Those virtues by which a man might become independent were much admired, i.e., thrift, prudence, hard work, frugality, and careful husbandry. It was once considered better to do without than to go into debt, and it is ever so that indebtedness increases dependence. The phrase that a male is "a man of his own" may now only evoke memories among older Americans, but it once meant that he had reached the age of twenty-one, was at liberty to seek his own well-being, and was *responsible* for providing for his needs. The family, at its best, encouraged personal independence by maintaining authority over those who forsook independence for its shelter. You could have independence or security, but not both. The community at large venerated self-reliance, individual initiative, personal independence, and individual achievement.

These were the primary foundations of American liberty.

3.

Undermining the Foundations

THE IDEAS WHICH would, in time, act as an acid to eat away the intellectual foundations of American liberty made their appearance and began to gain sway over thinkers in the period 1840-1890. Some of these corrosive ideas were not new, but whether new or old they gained impetus from new currents of thought which swept the intellectual world in the latter part of the nineteenth century. Few men living at that time realized that the ideas they were imbibing and sometimes championing would poison the roots of liberty. Few enough realize even today that they have done so.

Yet ideas, once accepted, follow their own internal logic to bend men and events toward their implicit ends, regardless of the intentions of those who hold them. Sticks and stones may break our bones, but words can be even more destructive—they can eat out the very life-giving marrow of the bone, leaving a hull which will crumble at the slightest blow. All of this occurs beneath the surface of the ordinary plane of our lives, which is why, when the direct attack upon liberty was made in the twentieth century, we were ill prepared to cope with it.

The task here is to reconstruct historically the way
in which new ideas entered the American mind in the
latter part of the nineteenth century and displaced
those which would have supported liberty. It is doubly
important that we do this. In the first place, it will help
to pin down the point at which Americans began to
stray from the path of liberty. And secondly, it will help
to sensitize us to those ideas and conceptions that are
antithetical to liberty.

There is no need to gloss over the fact that the history
of ideas is a difficult subject. The journey through it
can be likened to the fording of a stream with deep
waters lying all around and whirlpools swirling beneath
the placid surface to suck in the unwary. But there are
rewards that justify the effort: there is the pleasure of
the recognition of familiar noble ideas which were the
product of kindred minds and the at-first painful examination of one's own beliefs and assumptions. Most
important, it will help to provide that understanding
which is essential to the defense of liberty in this century of ideas and ideologies.

It will be remembered that American liberty was
based upon beliefs in the following: natural law, freedom of the mind and will, individual responsibility, and
rationalism. These in turn, to borrow from the verbiage
of the preceding chapter, were given evocative power
by the belief that there is a God who imbedded his immutable laws in the visible universe, that the individual
has a worth not measurable in human terms, that each
individual's good is inseparable from the general welfare, and that liberty is priceless for the individual and
socially beneficial. We will focus our attention, then,

upon the ideas which tended to undermine these foundations.

Romanticism vs. Reason

A test sample of the intellectual air which men
breathed in the middle of the nineteenth century would
likely show that the most active ingredient in it was
something that we now call romanticism. This romanticism was anything but opposed to individual liberty.
Rather, its outstanding spokesmen were probably the
most ardent proponents of freedom the world has ever
seen. Henry Thoreau refused to pay taxes to a government that acquiesced in the enslavement of human beings. Margaret Fuller wielded her pen in the cause of
the emancipation of women. Disciples could be found
for almost any cause that could lay claim to the purpose
of freeing either the body, mind, or spirit of man from
those things which fettered or bound it, whether it be
temperance, improved treatment of the insane, public
education, abolition of slavery, prison reform, emancipation of women, communitarianism, or shorter skirts for
women.

Ralph Waldo Emerson's thought can be used to exemplify this devotion to freedom that was typical of many
romantics. Emerson exhorted men to be free, to be self-
reliant, to plant themselves firmly in their own being,
and from that vantage point to stand with or against
other men as they were right or wrong. Self-reliance
was, after all, an essential prerequisite to the general
condition of liberty, but Emerson added new measure
to its meaning. A man not only ought to rely upon him-

self for the necessities of life, but he also ought to rely upon himself for the necessities of the spirit as well.

Emerson believed that knowledge could come by direct intuition, needing no intermediary for its perception. A man who would only have confidence in the eternal truth of that which came to him in this way might have that measure of it sufficient for his needs. To rely upon other men was to stifle the flow of knowledge and would lead only to pale imitation. Why take secondhand that which could be had in the exhilarating newness of personal discovery? Hark not to the voice of society, for it is "in conspiracy against the manhood of every one of its members."[1] Conform not to ancient usages unless they have personal relevance. Abjure the dictations of even intimate loved ones—father, mother, sister, wife—if they be contrary to the nature of the individual. "Whoso would be a man, must be a nonconformist." "What I must do," he said, "is all that concerns me, not what the people think."[2] It would be difficult to state a more uncompromising position on individual freedom.

The immediate impact of the romantic outlook, then, was favorable to individual liberty. Romantics usually venerated creativity and the uniqueness from which it springs, emphasized the importance of choice, opposed force, and stressed voluntarism. If each man was divine, as Walt Whitman said, then he was sacred and his person should be inviolate. No more comprehensive

---

[1] Ralph Waldo Emerson, "Self-Reliance," *Collected Works of Ralph Waldo Emerson* (New York: Greystone Press), p. 17.

[2] *Ibid.*, pp. 17-18.

belief could be summoned for the protection of the individual. Further, the romantic outlook rehabilitated faith and revived idealism.

But romanticism opened the door to beliefs which undercut the foundations of the belief in reason and natural law. As a movement, romanticism was, in part, a reaction to rationalism, or to its excesses. Romantics were less interested in law than in the spirit behind the law, much more concerned with Nature than with any state of nature, more likely to be subjective than objective. In their quest for the natural they were led backward to the primitive and primeval, to the irrational origins of habits, customs, and institutions. Their researches, studies, and imaginations drove them toward the conclusion that human activities and institutions rest upon desire, instinct, and custom rather than reason. And, since they had come to adore nature, they were precommitted to a preference for these irrational explanations.

European thinkers, particularly, were turning away from natural law and reason. Philosophers and scientists began to proclaim other grounds for human behavior. Schopenhauer, as one writer puts it, saw the prime mover of man as "Will, the dark and blind urge . . . , the will to live without any definite aim or purpose. . . ."[3] Nietzsche believed that the "will to power is the only meaning of life. . . ."[4] Freud exposed the power of the sexual urge in human behavior; Marx would ex-

---

[3] Hans Kohn, *The Twentieth Century* (New York: Macmillan, 1957), p. 47.

[4] *Ibid.*, p. 48

plain thought by the material conditions of society; Frazier explored the role of myth in social beliefs, and so on. In a stimulating study of the major European thinkers from 1890 to 1930, H. Stuart Hughes says, "Unquestionably the major intellectual innovators of the 1890's were profoundly interested in the problem of irrational motivation in human conduct. They were obsessed, almost intoxicated, with a rediscovery of the nonlogical, the uncivilized, the inexplicable."[5]

Darwinism

Into the midst of this disenchantment with reason came the Darwinian concept of evolution, the most stimulating intellectual discovery since the seventeenth century. No thinker of stature could avoid coming to terms with evolution, and many were soon embroiled in working out its implications. If accepted, the theory of evolution entailed a new conception of reality. It supplanted the stable, orderly, rational universe of Newton with an evolving, changing, nonrational universe. Change, not order, became the clue to understanding reality. Natural law—that is, a fixed order in the universe—became meaningless to a thoroughgoing Darwinian. Natural rights, if such a concept persevered, could have meaning only as they were related to a particular stage of evolution.

Darwinism offered the possibility, at least, of accounting for things without a creator. It offered a naturalistic account of the origin of life, of the source of change,

---

[5] H. Stuart Hughes, *Consciousness and Society* (New York: Alfred A. Knopf, 1958), p. 35.

and of the direction of development. It appeared that material objects could be accounted for in terms of their derivation from earlier material objects. Change took place by a gradual evolution.

Theories proliferated purporting to account for the force which produced change: such explanations as natural selection, sexual selection, the quest for available goods, and so forth. At any rate, matter and force were reckoned by many to be the most important constituents of reality. Even man himself was reduced to these constituents.

Jacques Loeb, a German biologist who came to America, said: "Living organisms are chemical machines consisting chiefly of colloidal material. . . ."[6] Ernst Haeckel held, as one historian describes it, that "man's mind as well as his body, together with all animal and vegetable species, has been evolved from protoplasm which arises from nitrogenous carbon compounds by spontaneous generation."[7] Lord Arthur Balfour declared, "Man, so far as natural science by itself is able to teach, is no longer the final cause of the universe, the Heaven-descended heir of all the ages. His very existence is an accident, his story a brief and transitory episode in the life of one of the meanest of the planets."[8]

While some of the above quotations are extreme, they do indicate the tendency of the impact of Darwinism

---

[6] Quoted in John H. Randall, Jr., *The Making of the Modern Mind* (Boston: Houghton Mifflin, 1940), p. 479.

[7] Carlton J. H. Hayes, *Contemporary Europe Since 1870* (New York: Macmillan, 1958), p. 207.

[8] Quoted in Randall, *op. cit.*, p. 581.

upon thought. Matter, force, change, relation, and primitive desire were replacing the belief in reason, order, permanency, and transcendental ideals. Some thinkers were reduced to a belief in the "persistence of force and the relativity of knowledge. . . ."[9] In short, when the Darwinian outlook was accepted and consistently followed, ideas dependent on the older view—natural rights, immutable law, human reason, the worth and dignity of man—had to be rejected.

It is one thing, however, to show that a few "advanced" European thinkers held certain ideas; it is quite another to show the general acceptance of these ideas in America. The logical tendency of an idea can be shown much more easily than can the fact that men made such interpretations. It is proper to doubt that such deep ideas have popular impact.

Yet leading American thinkers did, in time, shift with the current of Darwinian thought and accept its major tenets. (And this acceptance did in the course of time have a full impact upon American society, a point which will be more completely established in a later chapter.) There is now a considerable literature on the subject provided by intellectual historians. Anyone interested in tracing the influence of Darwinism on American thought should read either the whole or appropriate sections of the following: Richard Hofstadter's *Social Darwinism in American Thought,* Stow Persons' (editor) *Evolutionary Thought in America,* Stow Persons' *American Minds,* Oscar Cargill's *Intellectual America,* Alfred

---

[9] Richard D. Mosier, *The American Temper* (Berkeley: University of California Press, 1952), p. 251.

Kazin's *On Native Grounds,* and Richard D. Mosier's
The American Temper.

Our purposes can be served by indicating how Darwinism was used by Americans to undermine the beliefs
in freedom of the mind and will and of individual responsibility.

Individual liberty and individual responsibility are
premised upon the possibility of man originating and
controlling his behavior. It is essential to them that man
be the most important determinant in human action.
Darwinism, however, provided bases for ideas which
made of man an automaton, a mere twig, as it were,
caught in the current of a stream, driven by forces un-
controlled by him toward impersonally determined ends.
In short, evolutionary theories gave birth to or buttressed a host of deterministic theories: economic determinism, biological determinism, environmentalism,
naturalism, and social determinism, among others. It
did this by bolstering the organic conception of society,
the animality of man, the materiality of reality, and the
importance of external force.

Economic Determinism

Economic determinism was not new as a theory to
the latter part of the nineteenth century, but it was re-
formulated and given momentous aid by new currents
of thought. Karl Marx gave one of the most dogmatic
formulations of it. He maintained that the origin of the
structure of a society could be traced to the methods of
production carried on in that society, that these determined the social order, and that "it is not the con-

sciousness of men that determines their existence, but, on the contrary, their social existence determines their consciousness."[10] Marx declared that Darwin's discoveries provided him a basis in natural science, and books by Darwin and Marx were sold from the same shelf in socialist book stores.[11]

Economic determinism had its votaries in America, particularly by the beginning of the twentieth century. E. R. A. Seligman declared that to "economic causes must be traced in the last instance those transformations in the structure of society which themselves condition the relation of the social classes and the various manifestations of social life."[12] It was among historians, however, that the theory flourished. Brooks Adams tinged his account with a pessimistic fatalism, but saw economics as the key to civilization. But it was Charles A. Beard, with his seminal work, *An Economic Interpretation of the Constitution,* who drove the sword of economic determinism into the very heart of a major source of American liberty.

Biological determinism need not delay us much. Suffice it to say, this is the view that man's actions, thought, and development are determined or limited by his heredity. It did spur, among other things, the development of intelligence tests which are founded on the assumption

---

[10] Quoted in Morris Hillquit, *Socialism in Theory and Practice* (New York: Macmillan, 1909), p. 63.

[11] See Richard Hofstadter, *Social Darwinism in American Thought 1860-1915* (Philadelphia: University of Pennsylvania Press, 1944), p. 95.

[12] Quoted in Henry S. Commager, *The American Mind* (New Haven: Yale University Press, 1954), pp. 305-06.

of inherited capacity and limitations for learning. It also led to the investigations of glands which brook large in some explanations of behavior. But it was environmentalism which became the most important explanation of human behavior.

Environmentalism

The most extreme statement of environmentalism was made and popularized by an American, John B. Watson, in 1913 and the ensuing years. He called it behaviorism. The foundations for it were in the mechanistic and materialistic philosophies of the nineteenth century, however, and Watson's theory was bolstered by the results of the experiments in conditioning performed by the Russians, Vladimir M. Bekhterev and Ivan P. Pavlov. In brief, behaviorism is the belief that animal (including man's) behavior is the product of stimuli from the environment and the responses to them. So adequate was this explanation, Watson thought, that once sufficient human behavior had been observed, the behaviorist could, "given the stimulus . . . predict in advance what the response will be; or, given the response, he will be able to state what situation is calling out the reaction."[13] There is no room in such a theory for free will.

These ideas were brought to a wide audience by way of imaginative literature. This literature produced under the influence of deterministic theories is usually referred to as naturalistic. Naturalists consider man a product of his heredity and environment, an animal caught in

---

[13] "Behaviorism," *Encyclopaedia Britannica*, III, 328.

the powerful web of circumstances which he is power-less to overcome. As one writer says, "For the naturalists . . . men are 'human insects' whose brief lives are com-pletely determined by society or nature."[14] In America, naturalism was the dominant *motif* for Stephen Crane, Frank Norris, Theodore Dreiser, James Branch Cabell, Joseph Hergesheimer, Jack London, and James T. Farrell. Cabell put the importance of life in this way: "Living is a drab transaction, a concatenation of un-important events; man is impotent and aimless. . . ."[15]

There were many different interpretations of Darwin-ism, not all of them deterministic. And, it should be added, most Americans did not rush out to acquire and use these theories. Yet they did enter into the stream of American thought, and have practical import. Perhaps this entry can be demonstrated by the phenomenon known as "rugged individualism," a conception which originated in the latter part of the nineteenth century so far as I can make out.

Rugged Individualism

Rugged individualism was the bastard offspring of an illicit union between the belief in individual liberty and Darwinian evolution interpreted deterministically. On the surface, it appeared to be a continuation of Ameri-can individualism. Actually, however, it was flawed to its very core by determinism.

---

[14] Malcolm Cowley, "Naturalism in American Literature," *Evolutionary Thought in America,* Stow Persons, ed. (New York: George Braziller, 1956), p. 331.

[15] Quoted in Commager, *op. cit.,* p. 118.

This can be demonstrated by the thought of the leading American academic exponent of rugged individualism, William Graham Sumner. Sumner, who was a disciple of Herbert Spencer, made his initial impact as an exponent of liberty. He opposed attempts at governmental regulation of or interference with the economy, favored free trade and an absolute maximum of individual liberty, castigated reformers as impractical, and venerated individual responsibility.[16] Yet Sumner's views were increasingly vitiated by determinism. As he turned to the study of primitive societies, he moved toward a "rigidly deterministic view of societal evolution."[17] Sumner's own words show that he did not believe in man's freedom:

> The great stream of time and earthly things will sweep on just the same in spite of us. It bears with it now all the errors and follies of the past, the wreckage of all the philosophies, the fragments of all the civilizations, the wisdom of all the abandoned ethical systems, the debris of all the institutions, and the penalties of all the mistakes. It is only in imagination that we stand by and look at and criticize it and plan to change it. Every one of us is a child of his age and cannot get out of it. He is in the stream and is swept along with it.[18]

There is no purchase on rugged individualism from which to defend individual liberty. Individualism was

---

[16] See William Graham Sumner, *What Social Classes Owe to Each Other* (New York: Harper, 1920), *passim.*

[17] Hofstadter, *op. cit.*, pp. 133-34.

[18] William G. Sumner, "The Absurd Effort To Make the World Over," *American Thought: Civil War to World War I*, Perry Miller, ed. (New York: Rinehart, 1954), p. 104.

nothing more than a stage in the process of evolution. When conditions changed—those conditions which at that stage moved individuals to compete and to make progress—then a new organization of society would evolve and have to be accepted.

To the casual observer, American liberty must have appeared to be entrenched and secure in 1900. William McKinley, a man little apt to change the course of things, was re-elected to the Presidency. Social reformers were stymied: populism appeared to be dead; William Jennings Bryan, with some radical ideas, had been repudiated; Eugene Debs, with his tiny socialist following, hardly menaced the Republic. Yet beneath the surface the foundations of liberty were suffering erosions from the bombardment of new ideas. Americans were imbibing beliefs which could not be used in the defense of liberty.

Let us examine, imaginatively, attempting to defend liberty with the intellectual equipment that was being purveyed at the time. Suppose the individual when pressed to defend his liberty should claim that it was founded in natural right. But where in the changing universe of Darwinism would one find any basis for natural rights? Man never existed in a state of nature according to the latest anthropological findings, the man would be told. Rights are relative to the conditions of the time and the stage of evolution of the culture.

But surely, a man might argue, reason will support my rights. Already, however, there were men who taught that what appeared to be reason was nothing more than self-serving rationalization. Conscious thought plays too small a role in men's actual thought, said psychologists, to be granted much of a hearing. What really moves men is passion, desire, hunger, greed, and avarice. Americans were beginning to be taught to look beneath the stated reason for the "real" (i.e., subjective) explanation for what men said. Suppose a man were to give in and claim his liberties on the ground that he *desires* them, he would be defeated before he began. Where desire is the arbiter, when desires conflict, the appeal must be to force or power. In the United States, of course, the veiled force of the majority was substituted for the brute force of the mob.

In the new outlook, was there nothing to which the individual could appeal by right? No! Not in theory, though he might still be protected by the vestigial remains of liberties which had been institutionalized. Idealism has no place in a material universe; right is a useless concept in a world governed by force; voluntarism is a quaint notion if necessity actually rules in human affairs. There is no need to look for any protection for individual liberty in irrationalism, relativism, materialism, determinism, subjectivism, or organicism. It was these very ideas which undermined the foundations of liberty in America.

4.

Circumstances Hostile to Liberty

MEN BENT UPON tyranny will ever find means at hand for achieving it and justifications for imposing it. The unimaginative, the uncreative, the lazy, and the irresponsible can ever find formidable circumstances to excuse their failures. Whether any given set of circumstances is more favorable to liberty than another is debatable. It is not debatable, however, that conditions change, or that changed circumstances require different approaches to the same goal. Deterministic explanations of human behavior cannot be disposed of by simply denying any importance to circumstances. We front at any given time an imposing array of circumstances in terms of which we must modify our behavior or have it modified for us, react or respond, adjust to or overcome them. Effective action must proceed from an awareness both of enduring and of changing circumstances.

One of the inherent weaknesses of conservatism is its tendency to rely upon whatever is established and instituted, oblivious to the manifold changes that are occurring. At his best, the conservative labors to preserve enduring values; at his worst, he battles to maintain all established practices. Frequently, he stands for the ephemeral and enduring indiscriminately, thus laying himself open to the charge that he fears change and loves the comfort of the familiar. Quite likely, too, conservatives at any time will have among their number those who have established themselves in some favored position, and who wish to see it maintained as a special privilege.

Those whose dominant public concern is with liberty can make common cause with conservatives at one point—their desire to maintain instituted protections of liberty because it is an enduring value. But the task is not now one of simply maintaining liberty; it is in great measure one of restoring it. The posture of the indiscriminate conservative can be a positive hindrance in the latter undertaking. Liberty is a very practical matter. To ignore or gloss over changed circumstances will not help to maintain liberty, but it will play into the hands of those whose programs have resulted in a gradual circumscription of liberty. Twentieth century "liberals" have had the advantage too long of taking potshots at the conservative who would, they say, return to the days of McKinley.

The argument from circumstances (and the "necessity" of coming to terms with them) is the most powerful one in the arsenal of the "liberal." The argument cannot be countered either by ignoring or denouncing it. It can only be met effectively by recognizing the changed conditions of the twentieth century, acknowledging that changed circumstances require different approaches to liberty, and boldly confronting these circumstances with new ideas and programs. An historical purpose can be served also by calling attention to the changed physical conditions in America, for it was in terms of them that reformers advanced their programs and infused America with their ideas.

It is not necessary to embrace a deterministic environmentalism in order to recognize that changed circumstances can alter the conditions of individual liberty. When conditions are simple, the alternatives for choice are more apparent. The fewer people involved in a decision the easier it is for all of them to participate effectively in the decision-making process. Economic independence promotes individual liberty; dependence is a deterrent. As the situation becomes more complex, as men's lives become more interrelated, as institutions grow in size and complexity, as organizations extend their reach, liberty becomes ever more difficult to maintain. Conversely, it is much easier for tyranny to be subtly extended.

Conditions of the American Frontier

The foundations of American liberty were conceived and laid in an overwhelmingly rural, agrarian, sparsely populated, and informal America. These foundations rested upon premises inherited from the Old World and practices congenial to the New World conditions. There is, of course, no conclusive proof that the belief in individual liberty was simply a product of the American environment, and I doubt that it was. New soil can become the ground for new tyrannies if men are willing. My assumption is that the devotion to liberty grows out of faith, hope, belief, and determination before which conditions may be nothing more than an adjunct.

At any rate, New World conditions offered opportunities congenial to the development of liberty if men's minds were bent in that direction. This new land offered to the settlers unbounded opportunity to conquer, to build, to change, to create a country, as it were, to their own liking. Early settlers were largely free from the binding fetters of custom, from the necessity to conform to established ways, from many of the prescriptions of class and caste, from most, if not all, of the limitations of an established order.

But the New World not only offered much; it also required much of the settlers. It required strength, courage, ingenuity; it placed great responsibility upon the individual: he must establish order, and he must provide for himself and his own or perish.

So, for intellectual, spiritual, and circumstantial reasons, Americans developed an order in which there was much individual liberty and a corresponding individual responsibility. Social customs arose to abate the loneliness and ameliorate the severity of individual responsibility. They tended to be voluntary in character, and to depend upon cooperation rather than coercion for their working. I have in mind such folkways and customs as house-raisings, house-warmings, hog-killings, quilting bees, cornhuskings, and sitting up with the sick and the dead. In case of severe need occasioned by crop failure, hail, being burned out, the loss of an indispensable cow or horse, neighbors frequently made up an offering to help out. It was customary in the nineteenth century for orphans, the aged, the infirm, the crippled, and the maimed to be cared for by the closest kin among the relatives. When death occurred, the neighbors not only sat up during the period of mourning but also laid out the body, built the coffin as likely as not, dug the grave, and sang at the funeral. Recreation originated in and was participated in by the community: singings, all-day to-do's, cakewalks, square dances, turkey shoots, fox hunts, debates, fish fries, and picnics.

Rural Americans, that is most Americans before the Civil War, produced most of the necessities of life on the farm and in the home. They grew most of their food, hunted and fished for a portion of their meat, spun their yarn, wove and fashioned homespun clothes, churned their butter, made their soap and the lye that went into it. A family often "got by" with only an occasional trip to the store to purchase spices, salt, powder and shot, and delicacies or trinkets. The farmer was by necessity a jack-of-all-trades, adept at everything from carpentry to wood splitting. The farm wife was expected to be accomplished in everything from fancy needlework to gardening.

I describe neither utopia nor pastoral bliss. There was much hard and lonely work, much suffering; the rains fell on the just and the unjust alike. My point is that here were people who had a way of life built upon independence, who had a significant liberty to dispose of their time and resources, and were profoundly aware of their responsibilities for their own well-being. Self-respect and community respect depended upon maintaining independence. There was something even shameful in having to ask aid of anyone else. Help from others should be volunteered, not asked for.

The Civil War can be and often has been taken as the dividing line between the old and the new America— as that point at which such diverse and multitudinous

changes began to spread across America that we can
profitably speak of a qualitative change in the conditions of American life. As one historian states it, "Our
nation of 1865 was a nation of farmers, city artisans,
and industrious independent business men, and small
scale manufacturers. . . . In this period before the Civil
War comparatively small single owners, or frequently
copartnerships, controlled practically every industrial
field."[1] After the Civil War there emerged an increasingly industrialized, urbanized, and mechanized America.

Changes After the Civil War

It is neither practical nor necessary to trace out in
detail the multitudinous changes that have occurred
affecting the condition of Americans since the Civil
War. It will be useful, however, to consider some of
them in detail and to suggest the impact of others. I
shall focus upon those developments which have been
attended by increasing dependency, ramifying inter-
dependency, growing complexity, and a circumscription
of the area of choice of the individual. My purpose will
be threefold: to show that the conditions within which
liberty could possibly be maintained have changed,
to indicate the bearing of changes upon the individual's
view of his chances for free choice, and to lay bare the
circumstantial background which made "liberal" programs appear necessary and desirable.

While the Civil War and developments attendant
upon it did not start the train of events and develop-

---

[1] Burton J. Hendrick, *The Age of Big Business* (New
Haven: Yale University Press, 1919), pp. 2-3, 6-7.

ments which were to circumscribe the individual, it did accentuate and accelerate some of them. The outcome of the war practically determined that the union was indissoluble, that states having once joined it were subject to national decisions. The constitutional amendments adopted in consequence of the war greatly extended the scope of the central government. The Fourteenth Amendment made citizenship national, forbade states to violate the privileges of any citizen (thus laid the foundation for federal courts to provide rights). The Fifteenth Amendment extended the role of the national government into the determination of who should vote. The war and reconstruction made force a part of the character of the United States; no one could now correctly maintain that the union was voluntary. The extension of the powers of the national government created a greater force at a further remove from the individual, made government more impersonal, and made it less likely that an individual could alter its course.

The difficulties of the freed Negro may demonstrate to some extent the difficulties of achieving liberty in that postwar United States. On the face of it, the freeing of the Negro was a gain for liberty in the United States. But most Negroes were unprepared for this giant step into freedom, and the hard truth is that they frequently traded slavery for peonage. Much of their newfound freedom was lost in the share-crop and supply system which emerged in the South to replace the slave-plantation system. By the end of the nineteenth century the Negro, more often than not, was politically disfranchised, socially segregated, and economically encumbered. He became one of the several elements of the population receptive to the appeal of government-provided "independence."

A Changing Agriculture

If the Negro made some gains relative to his former condition, the white people in the South lost in independence during and after Reconstruction. Both as a result of governmental attempts to make over the South and because of the fall in prices of farm products, many white men were reduced to tenant farming. The trend toward white tenancy mounted through the years. "In 1900 about 36 per cent of all white farmers in Dixie belonged to these classes. In 1930 the proportion had gone up . . . to about 45 per cent."[2] Negroes and whites became competitors at the same level for the available land.

The Southern white man alleviated, to some extent, the threat of submergence by the Negro by developing industries which were usually closed to the Negro. But in so doing the Southerner frequently traded the dependence of the tenant for that of the factory and mine-worker. If anything, the factory worker was more dependent upon the mill operator than the tenant had been upon the landlord. Frequently he lived in a company house, bought necessities at the company store, was "protected" by the company police, sent his children to the company school, and attended a church subsidized by the company.

The national agricultural situation followed a simi-

---

[2] Wilbur J. Cash, *The Mind of the South* (Garden City: Doubleday, 1954), p. 283.

lar, though less dramatic, pattern. The farmer's independence was being drained away by declining prices, heavy shipping and machinery costs, and increasing indebtedness. In the 1890's, 27 per cent of American farms were mortgaged, and by 1910 the proportion had increased to 33 per cent. Farm tenantry was rising nationally: in 1880, 25 per cent of American farms were cultivated by tenants; by 1910 the figure had risen to 37 per cent.[3]

The period from 1865 to 1890 had been one of unprecedented agricultural and westward expansion (a major reason for the surplus in farm products which drove prices downward), of the occupation of new lands, of gold and silver rushes, of the building of cattle empires and the massacre of buffalo for their hides, of the expropriation of resources and the filling out of the West. Opportunity did not end abruptly in 1890, but the surface resources that had drawn men westward were owned and being utilized. The fertile land had been claimed; the range land was being fenced; the buffalo had been killed. Some Americans became aware that our resources were not limitless, and Congress passed the first conservation laws. This change in conditions set the stage for the belief that the ownership and control of property—and its use and abuse—by some men was a threat to others.

Momentous economic changes occurred between 1865 and 1900. It was a period of rampant rugged individualism, of the accumulation of great fortunes in steel,

---

[3] T. Harry Williams, Richard N. Current and Frank Friedel, *A History of the United States* (New York: Alfred A. Knopf, 1959), II, 172-79.

meat, oil, silver, and rails, of the concentration of wealth
in the hands of powerful individuals, of the spanning
of the continent by railroad and telegraph, of wild stock
market coups, of prosperity and depression. According
to one report, the wealthiest man in New York was
worth $6 million in 1855. When Cornelius Vanderbilt
died in 1877, he left a fortune of $104 million. Andrew
Carnegie sold his steel interests in the early twentieth
century for stocks and bonds valued at $492 million.[4]

Rugged Individualists

Many rugged individualists used their wealth and
manipulative skill to form monopolies and trusts. When
Standard Oil Company, the first great trust, was formed
in 1870 there were twenty-five independent refineries in
Cleveland. In two years Standard absorbed all but five
of these. "By 1874 the greatest refineries in New York
and Philadelphia had likewise merged their identity
with his [Rockefeller's] own. When Rockefeller began
his acquisition, there were thirty independent refineries
operating in Pittsburgh, all of which, in four or five
years, passed one by one under his control. The largest
refineries of Baltimore surrendered in 1875."[5] Thus did
smaller enterprises succumb to absorption by the giants.

It is doubtful that individuals acting alone would
have been able to gain virtual control of whole industries. Rockefeller combined his wealth and acumen with
that of other men to form his predatory trust. Many of
the great railroads were built with funds subscribed by

---

[4] Hendrick, *op. cit.*, pp. 10, 19, 84.
[5] *Ibid.*, p. 36.

numerous individuals, groups, towns, and states. Furthermore, while governments rarely interfered with business operations in the late nineteenth century, they did actively aid and assist them in a variety of ways. There were tariffs, patents, franchises, and injunctions available to the fortunate, and some railroads received large grants of land and huge government loans. Combinations of capital could operate throughout the United States under the frequently uninhibitory charters of a single state. The courts, instead of acting to limit the activities of combinations, extended their protection over them: the Supreme Court ruled *(Santa Clara Co.* v. *Southern Pacific R.R. Co.)* that a corporation was a person in the sense implied in the Fourteenth Amendment. It was these conditions—government aid and protection with a minimum of restriction—which made possible the great concentrations of wealth and power.[6]

Following upon and accompanying industrialization and the nationalization of business was a tremendous increase in nonagricultural and industrial workers. In 1860 there were 4,325,116 nonagricultural workers in the United States; in 1900 there were 18,161,235, a more than fourfold increase. Whatever else may be said for the "blue collar" and "white collar" workers, who made up an increasing proportion of these nonagricul-

---

[6] I refrain from entering into the debate as to whether these developments produced more "good" or "evil." Such questions are usually answered within a framework of assumptions—pragmatic, materialistic, and the belief that man has sufficient knowledge to make such judgments—which I do not share. My interest in these developments here is restricted to them as they became circumstances of liberty.

tural laborers, they were usually dependent and exposed when depressions and layoffs came. More often than not, they had neither land, property, nor insurance to fall back upon in adversity. Moreover, employment was uncertain: it fluctuated drastically in depressions such as those of the 1870's and 1890's (not to mention the 1930's), and in recessions in 1884, 1893, and 1907. Financial panics and depressions were not new to this time, but their impact was much more widespread and devastating than it had been in an earlier America when men were apt to be less dependent upon one another.

Urbanization

Accompanying and related to industrialization and the increase of industrial workers was the rise of the city in the late nineteenth century. Though rural still outnumbered urban inhabitants, one historian says: "In America in the eighties urbanization for the first time became a controlling factor in national life. Just as the plantation was the typical product of the *antebellum* Southern system and the small farm of the Northern agricultural order, so the city was the supreme achievement of the new industrialism."[7]

So many problems which concern only the individual or the family in rural areas are a common and collective concern in the city. If a farmer in a rural area has a pigpen near the house, only he and his family are likely to suffer, but for a man to keep pigs in the city may

[7] Arthur M. Schlesinger, *The Rise of the City* (New York: Macmillan, 1933), p. 79.

offend the nostrils of all those within a city block. City life provided the circumstantial background for much of the regulatory legislation of the twentieth century, which increasingly circumscribed the liberty of the individual.

Urban living has affected liberty, too, by obscuring the reality within which American liberty was conceived. The farmer is in daily contact with a reality of conditions which he did not create and some of which he is impotent to alter. The rains fall or the drought deepens; the frost comes early or the hail destroys the crops. The city dweller lives in contact with no such obvious constraining reality. The conditions of his existence are mostly man-made, hence apparently alterable at will. He is easy prey to the idea that he alone creates wealth, or that whatever is wrong can be corrected by governmental action. He seeks scapegoats in adversity and worships heroes in prosperity. If the farmer too is susceptible to these attitudes, it may be indicative of the fact that he derives more and more of his opinions from the city via the mass media of communication.

The few developments I have discussed in some detail are only a beginning and a sampling of that totality of circumstances that surround the individual in the twentieth century. The huge immigration that poured into America in the late nineteenth and early twentieth century swelled the population of Eastern cities with near destitute inhabitants, many of them illiterate even in their own tongues, having come from lands without traditions of representative government, used to paternalistic arrangements, and whose conception of democracy was frequently vitiated with socialism and anarchism. Enterprising individuals in the early twentieth century sometimes found the sources of capital closed to them by a virtual "money trust."[8] An international order which had generally kept the peace in the nineteenth century swiftly deteriorated in the twentieth, and we have been confronted with total war and its attendant circumscription of the liberty of the individual. The development of the mass media of communication has provided means for subtle and vulgar manipulation of the individual—both by governments and by private concerns—unprecedented in the history of man. Standardization, rationalization, and mechanization are abstractions standing for practices used by ever larger organizations in the twentieth century to alter the context within which human liberty could be realized.

It is to simplify, but there is much validity to the view that the individual has been dwarfed by nationalized, consolidated, and centralized businesses; swallowed up in giant corporations, vast bureaucracies, and huge armies; battered by total war, economic depressions, governmental and business propaganda; made apparently insignificant by his life in impersonal cities; replaced by the machine, or required to adjust to its demands; baffled by the complexity of the operations in

---

[8] The "money trust" was a term used in the early twentieth century to describe the dominant position of the Rockefellers and Morgan of major American financial institutions. The Pujo Committee reported in 1913: "If by a 'money trust' is meant an established and well-defined identity and community of interest between a few leaders of finance . . . your committee . . . has no hesitation in asserting . . . that the condition thus described exists in this country to-day." [Quoted in Harold U. Faulkner, *The Quest for Social Justice* (New York: Macmillan, 1931), pp. 46-47.]

the world in which he lives; manipulated by salesmen, advertisers, politicians, announcers, and assorted confidence men.

Safety Sought in Numbers

How has he reacted or responded to these pressures and conditions? In the broadest terms, the response can be suggested figuratively. To begin, man acts in a strange and sometimes irrational but an almost always consistent manner when confronted by forces that are, or appear to be, beyond his control. He seeks company in his fear and impotence, to lose himself within some group or in the mass of humanity, to submerge himself in something larger than himself. What man, confronted by some natural phenomenon posing a threat to himself—say an oncoming storm—has not wished for the warmth and companionship of the family circle? It is the gathering of friends which assuages the pangs of grief when some member of the family is claimed by death.

The developments we have been considering do not appear upon analysis to be natural phenomena. But they took on something of the same sort of inevitable coloration. It was the relative incomprehensibility of the developments which made them so formidable to the individual. What man does not comprehend, he cannot control. Furthermore, that which is beyond the individual's comprehension appears to be a force beyond the control of man. Giant corporations, complex mechanical operations, big government which could be heard and felt but not seen, made it appear that these behemoths acted with a will of their own, resisting the interference of a mere man. Probably these conditions came nearer to convincing men that things were determined outside of and beyond their control than any subtle theory could have done.

Men reacted, then, by joining together in groups: labor unions, business associations, secret societies, patriotic organizations, pressure groups, farm organizations, and cooperatives. These, in turn, became a menace to individual liberty. Witness, for example, the plight of the unorganized worker as an individual pitted against the combined force of organized men in a union. This condition added more fuel to the fire of demands for government mediation and regulation.

This account is only in part valid. The story of man differs from that of the story of lower animals. Man does not simply react to circumstances; he formulates theories and explanations and acts upon them. He is guided and directed by his interpretations, beliefs, and assumptions. It is *not* my contention that the course that American history took was inevitable nor that it was simply a reaction to circumstances. On the contrary, circumstances provided the favorable soil for the seeds of ideas planted by reformers of the time we have been considering. Conditions lent an air of plausibility to interpretations that were made of them. My point here is that there were new circumstances that posed problems for traditional concepts of American liberty, that these conditions provided a backdrop for reform efforts, and that failure to take them fully into account by defenders of liberty has led us into the present morass.

5.

A Collectivist

Curvature of the Mind

ANY CAPABLE OBSERVER should be able to see that there has been a gradual and mounting circumscription of liberty in America in the twentieth century. It manifests itself in the spreading tenacles of government control and regulation, in the concentration of power in the federal government, in government by presidential decree, in the unchecked rulings of independent commissions, in the proliferating activities of government agencies, in the virtual confiscation of earnings by means of the progressive income tax, and by a diminishing control of their property by owners.

Complaints about the increasing role of government in what were once the private affairs of citizens, about the attrition of individual liberty and of family, local, community, and state control of affairs, are met with a chorus of replies which are larded with such terms as "necessary," "inevitable," "destined," "realistic," and "practical." Note, for example, the tenor of this recent announcement from the White House. "We are going to have an urban department," said John F. Kennedy. "It may not come this year, but in my opinion, it will be-

come as *necessary* and *inevitable* as the Department of
Agriculture and HEW."[1] Many writers and speakers imply by their language that the momentous changes of
this century have occurred as a result of ineluctable
processes that were beyond the will and control of man,
that the centralization of government, for instance, was
born by immaculate conception out of necessitous circumstances.[2]

So far wide of the mark is this interpretation of the
changes of this century as products of circumstances
that it amounts to a major distortion of history. In fact,
the turning to government to solve every problem, the
extension of government regulation and control, the
provision of government aid, result from a bent of the
American mind. Not only did this curvature of the
mind not grow simply out of circumstances but, on the
contrary, it was implanted by theorists, novelists, and
assorted reformers. That ideas derived from this curvature of the mind now appear "natural" and "inevitable"
is not particularly strange; it is the recurrence of a phenomenon that has occurred time and time again in his-

---

[1] *Time*, LXXIX (March 23, 1962), p. 16. Italics mine.

[2] In the first chapter of *The New Age of Franklin Roosevelt
1932-1945* (Chicago: University of Chicago Press, 1957),
Professor Dexter Perkins refers to "the *necessity* for the
regulation of their affairs by government," "the *need* for control," a "point of view of the problem of relief that was
destined to be accepted," a question that is "*inevitably* complex," "the *need* for relief appropriations," and "*justifiable*
to meet the *needs* of relief. . . . " He argues, in the second
chapter, "that the New Deal had its *roots in social circumstances* and is more wisely regarded as the reaction of the
Americans to the Great Depression rather than as the accomplishment . . . of any individual." (p. 71.) Italics mine.

tory—the phenomenon of the acceptance by those who do not analyze their beliefs of whatever is established and usual as natural and right.

There was a time not so very long ago, however, when those ideas imbedded in the national consciousness by the New Nationalism, the New Freedom, the New Deal(s), and the Fair Deal were new and untried, when they appeared as ridiculous to men of power and influence as any other ideas do now. This means nothing more (nor less) than that the collectivist curvature of the mind has now become an orthodoxy. My point, however, is that those ideas which now hold sway over Americans were spread by men. They were formulated into theories by writers and speakers, propagated by reformers and politicians, served as ideological ballast for programs and movements, and are believed by many Americans because they were taught to them.[3]

In earlier chapters, I have attempted to explain how the way was prepared for a new ethos in America. The intellectual foundations of liberty—belief in reason, freedom of the mind and will, natural law, and individual responsibility—were undermined by deterministic theories bolstered by Darwinism, by an increasing emphasis upon the role of the nonrational in human behavior, and by doctrines of force and necessity. Industrialization and mechanization, accompanied by the rise of the city, the influx of numerous immigrants from Southern and Eastern Europe, the concentration of

---

[3] It should be said, in justice, that there is a considerable body of scholarly literature today analyzing the ideas of reform and showing how they came to inform Americans. But this has been ill taught thus far by historians at large.

wealth, and the growth of corporations and trusts posed new problems for the livelihood and independence of the individual.

Darwinism provided the ideas for a new outlook. At first, Darwinism was used to preserve the existing order with its individualistic orientation. Men like William Graham Sumner and Andrew Carnegie took such ideas as natural selection and survival of the fittest and described them as the means by which social progress was wrought out of individual effort. Sumner, as I have shown, used the ideas of gradual evolution and the determining role of social custom and practice in human affairs as an argument against the possibility of reform. But Sumner's individualism was vitiated by determinism, his quest for freedom turned into the extolling of necessity, and the basic ideas from which he had drawn his defense became a springboard for the collectivistic interpretations which abounded among thinkers in the late nineteenth century. In short, reform-minded thinkers worked out a justification for reform which they based on Darwinian evolution. Some historians refer to such reform theories as reform Darwinism.[4]

The collectivist ethos—viewed as a coherent philosophy—resulted from the mingling and mutation of ideas drawn from many sources. It has become by now a kind of "American" ideology. Properly speaking, it is neither socialism, nor communism, nor capitalism. Its adherents prefer to call it democracy or, when they are in a more descriptive frame of mind, social democracy. Thus far, the application of this ideology in America

---

[4] Eric F. Goldman, *Rendezvous with Destiny* (New York: Vintage Books, 1956), ch. V.

has eventuated in the creation of a partial welfare state. It supports a tendency toward some kind of national socialism within a framework of international (excluding the communist sphere) socialism, and the United States is listing heavily in that direction at present. To trace this ideology back to its sources is to expose the eclectic means by which it was formed. But this should not mislead us as to its present condition as a total ideology whose adherents now accept and propagate without doubt or thought.

The collectivist curvature of the mind owes its bent most directly to the conception of society as an organism. Briefly stated, this is the view that society—far from being merely a collection of individuals—has a being of its own. In the thought of collectivists, society is "thingified," has a life and needs of its own, is the source of "human" being, and, presumably, is the end for which man exists. To show that the existence of such a conception is not a figment of my imagination, permit me to quote from some of those who spread it. Lester Frank Ward, a pioneer American sociologist and seminal social thinker, said:

> The individual has reigned long enough. The day has come for society to take *its affairs* into *its own hands* and shape *its own destinies.*[5]

And again:

> But society must be looked upon in the light of a conscious individual. Insofar as it is conscious and

---

[5] "Sociocracy," *American Thought: Civil War to World War I*, Perry Miller, ed. (New York: Rinehart, 1954), p. 113. Italics mine.

in proportion to the completeness of its consciousness, it does not differ from an individual. No individual ever limits his activities to the simple sphere of self-preservation. Every individual is always seeking to benefit himself in every possible way. Society should do the same. . . . The extent to which it will do this will depend upon the collective intelligence. This is to society what brain power is to the individual. . . .[6]

Frederick Jackson Turner, who attempted to explain American history in terms of physical environment, and did spread the idea of the end of the frontier, declared:

Society is an organism, ever growing. History is the self-consciousness of this organism. . . .[7] First we recognize why all the spheres of man's activity must be considered. Not only is this the only way in which we can get a complete view of the society, but no one department of social life can be understood in isolation from the others. . . . Therefore, all kinds of history are essential . . . ; all are truly parts of *society's endeavor* to understand *itself* by understanding *its* past.[8]

Henry George, the pace-setter and pathfinder of reformers, betrays his organic conception of society with these words:

The rude society resembles the creatures that though cut into pieces will live; the highly civilized society is like a highly organized animal. . . .[9]

---

[6] Lester F. Ward, *Applied Sociology* (Boston: Ginn and Co., 1906), pp. 38-39.

[7] Fritz Stern (ed.), "An American Definition of History," *The Varieties of History*, (Cleveland: World Publishing Co., 1956), p. 203.

[8] *Ibid.*, p. 201. Italics mine.

[9] "Social Problems," *American Thought*, p. 50.

Note, in the choice of language exercised by Woodrow Wilson, how this conception had entered into the stream of political thought:

> The trouble with the theory [of a Constitution based on natural law with checks and balances] is that government is not a machine, but a living thing. It falls, not under the theory of the universe, but under the theory of organic life. . . . Living political constitutions must be Darwinian in structure and in practice. Society is a living organism and must obey the laws of life. . . .
>
> All that progressives ask or desire is permission—in an era when "development," "evolution," is the scientific word—to interpret the Constitution according to the Darwinian principle; all they ask is recognition of the fact that a nation is a living thing and not a machine.[10]

The central concept of the complex of ideas which increasingly dominates American thought, then, is the organic conception of society. It is the hard core of the ideology which has informed the twentieth century reform effort. The organic conception was derived mainly from Darwinism, by analogic extrapolation of ideas arrived at from the biological data with which Darwin dealt. It has been variously envisioned and applied by different thinkers.

Thus, to Theodore Roosevelt the social organism was the nation. Attend to the revealing terminology with which he spoke:

> *National* efficiency has many factors. It is a neces-

---

[10] Woodrow Wilson, *The New Freedom*, William E. Leuchtenburg, intro. and notes (Englewood Cliffs: Prentice-Hall, 1961), p. 42.

sary result of the principle of conservation widely applied. In the end it will determine our *failure* or *success as a nation*. National efficiency has to do, not
only with natural resources and with men, but it is
equally concerned with institutions. . . . It is a misfortune when the national legislature fails to do its
duty in providing a *national remedy*, so that the only
national activity is the purely negative activity of the
judiciary. . . .[11]

He refers elsewhere to "national rights."[12] This way
of thinking has entered into the writing and speaking
habits of Americans, and now we encounter casual references to national resources, national income, national
wealth, national purpose, national problems, national
vigor, and human resources (of the nation).

Other thinkers broaden the organic conception so
that it embraces all the peoples of the earth. Would-be-
president Adlai Stevenson expresses such an extension
in this quotation:

The purpose of our aid programs should therefore
be designed not primarily to counter communism—
though it will do this too—but to create conditions of
self-respect and self-sustaining growth in economies
still behind the threshold of modernization. . . . I believe that this is the chief way to [sic] us to extend our
vision of "a more perfect union" to all mankind. It is
a commonplace that in a world made one by science
and the atom, the old national boundaries are dis-
solving, the old landmarks vanishing. . . . A workable
human society has to be fashioned and we must start

[11] Theodore Roosevelt, *The New Nationalism*, William E.
Leuchtenburg, intro. and notes (Englewood Cliffs: Prentice-
Hall, 1961), pp. 35-36. Italics mine.
[12] *Ibid.*, p. 43.

where we can—by setting up the institutions of a *common economic life,* by employing our wealth and wisdom to spark the growth of production in poorer lands, by working together with like-minded powers to establish the permanent patterns of a workable *world economy.*[13]

On the other hand, John Dewey, the philosophical catalyst who wove together the many strains of reform thought into an ideology, applied the organic conception to ideas and ideologized democracy. To Dewey—if I may quote my own summation of his ideas—"democracy is a political system, an economic system, a social system, and an educational system. It is a criterion for judgments, a theory of knowledge, a method, a principle, an aim, an ideal, a thing in itself. It is a way of life, a form of life, a form of associated living, a guide for living, a matter of faith. It is equalitarian, humanistic, scientific, concerned with the needs and wants of man, constantly changing and growing. It calls for a particular kind of organization of society and a particular orientation of all aspects of the culture . . .," and "there is the nondescriptive usage . . .—democracy as an agreed-upon value which is to be realized in the society, an unquestioned good."[14] The above ideas, too, are the basic ones of the prevailing ideology.

It is not whim that prompts me to give so much em-

[13] "Extend Our Vision . . . to all Mankind," *The National Purpose* (New York: Holt, Rinehart and Winston, 1960), pp. 32-33. Italics mine.

[14] Clarence B. Carson, "The Concept of Democracy and John Dewey," *Modern Age* (Spring 1960), p. 184. See Appendix.

phasis to the organic conceptions of society and of ideas. For it is beliefs drawn from these that have crowded out the belief in individual liberty. American thinkers did not so much disavow individual liberty (though they frequently condemned individualism) as they accepted ideas which displaced and subordinated it to other beliefs. After all, once the mind has been curved to think in terms of such grandiose conceptions as national purpose, the fabric of society, the unity of peoples, the needs and desires of mankind, individual liberty can be, and has been, made to appear pale and insignificant beside them. How incommensurable are individual liberty and the "good of mankind" when they are portrayed as in conflict with one another! This was especially the case as individual liberty picked up overtones, within the collectivistic ethos, of selfishness, acquisitiveness, and narrowness. But, in the main, individual liberty was shunted aside, not overcome by direct assault.

Many another ideational twig was grafted on to the ideological tree of the organic conception of society before it bore collectivistic fruits. The religion of humanity—partly temporalized Christianity and mostly refurbished humanism—provided the moral fervor and ethical imperatives to collectivism. As one historian describes it, this religion of humanity comprised the following views, among others.

Its root lies in universal human nature; because of this common root, historical religions are all one. . . . Its moving power is faith in man as a progressive being. Its objective is the perfection or complete development of man, the race serving the individual, and the individual the race. Its practical work is to humanize the world. . . .[15]

Environmentalism was grafted on to collectivism to serve as explanation of human behavior. But this new ethos avoided absolute determinism. The claims of determinism were shaken for many twentieth-century thinkers by the "radical" freedom of William James. It was radical because James not only denied that man's behavior is determined by external forces, but also denied that there were any fixed and immutable laws in the universe. At any rate, reformers turned to the meliorism of Lester Frank Ward, who accepted the large role which society and environment play in human behavior, but argued that men, acting collectively, could control social development.

Relativism

Collectivists used relativism to undermine the prevailing certainties. They deified the "common man" and hypostatized, as I have already shown, the democracy through which he was supposed to speak. They called for a positive role for government, which should act forcefully as the "arm" of society to achieve the aims of the "people." Thinkers redefined rights so that they became "positive" rather than "negative" concepts. For example, John Dewey defined liberty as "power, effective power to do specific things. There is no such thing as liberty in general; liberty, so to speak, at large.

---

[15] Ralph H. Gabriel, *The Course of American Democratic Thought* (New York: Ronald Press, 1956), p. 187.

. . . The moment one examines the question from the standpoint of effective action, it becomes evident that the demand for liberty is a demand for power. . . ."[16] Thus defined, liberty becomes a claim for effective power, and, since Americans were entitled to liberty, it became a claim upon government to provide the citizenry with power.

Many other ideas have found lodging in this collectivistic ideology, though some of them are not firmly fixed. The belief in science and scientism is fairly deeply embedded in it. Sometimes class ideas are stronger than the organic conception of society, and some collectivists —those nearest to the Marxist tradition, usually—find the depository of virtue to be not so much in the "common man" as the laboring man, or simply "labor." Strangely, too, elitist ideas—though described in a different language—have found their way into this ideology. Thus, we find collectivists venerating experts and joining in the call for leaders. And, of course, social planning and human control appear to be firmly fixed in this ethos, as does equalitarianism.

In making my account of the curvature of the mind, thus far, I have tried to make clear that we are dealing with ideas formulated by men, not some magical transformation thrust upon us by fate. I want to go further and point up the fact that the spread of these ideas and the impetus to reform came from men and groups, not, as Professor Dexter Perkins says of the New Deal, from "a social process arising out of depression. . . ."[17]

---

[16] John Dewey, *Problems of Men* (New York: Philosophical Library, 1946), p. 111.
[17] Perkins, *op. cit.*, p. 80.

In the first place, these reform ideas were formulated and spread by theorists. Henry George, a leader among these, published *Progress and Poverty* in 1879. It is estimated that by 1905 more than two million copies had been sold in the United States and elsewhere.[18] The cause of the evils in America, George declared, was the private appropriation of rent—the unearned increment from land. His solution: take all rents by way of a single government tax, and the situation will right itself. George's specific proposal made no long range impact, but his covert attack upon property, his declamations against existing conditions, his proposals to use government for social purposes, have left a deep mark.

The major reform ideas which were to go into the new ideology received their early articulation in the writings of Lester Frank Ward in the late nineteenth and early twentieth centuries. His central works were *Psychic Factors in Civilization, Dynamic Sociology, Pure Sociology,* and *Applied Sociology.* He opened the way for reform, theoretically, by arguing that a new stage in evolution had been reached, a stage in which society could take over the direction of its development by using "social intelligence."

In this new stage, mind had repealed "the law of nature, and enacted in its stead the psychologic law, or law of mind."[19] He advanced the notion that feelings are the source of ideas. "The true order of the phenomena is that the conditions arouse the feelings and the feelings create the ideas or beliefs. These last are the final

---

[18] Gabriel, *op. cit.,* p. 212.
[19] Commager, *op. cit.,* p. 206.

form into which the whole is crystallized in the human mind, constituting the thought of the age and people in which they prevail. . . ."[20] He redefined justice and equality. "The true definition of justice is that it is the enforcement by society of an artificial equality in social conditions that are naturally unequal. By it the strong are forcibly shorn of their power to exploit the weak."[21] The hedonistic strain in the new thought was made explicit: "The new ethics has for its aim the minimization of pain and the maximization of pleasure."[22]

Of Ward's influence, Commager says: "He inspired a whole generation of scholars and reformers to believe that it was possible to remake society along happier lines, and a new generation that did not know him worked with his tools and fought with his weapons."[23]

Thorstein Veblen worked to construct an evolutionary view of economics, an economics no longer "inhibited" by fixed laws. Justice Oliver Wendell Holmes, Jr., wrenched the interpretation of constitutional law out of the path of its "subservience" to the Constitution or to natural law, belabored his colleagues for making decisions based upon their social and economic assumptions, and implied that judges should bow to the will of the majority.[24]

Henry Demarest Lloyd denounced the depredations of private wealth and public corporations and held out the lure of solution to the problems which beset America

---

[20] Ward, *op. cit.*, p. 47.

[21] *Ibid.*, p. 23.

[22] *Ibid.*, p. 28.

[23] Commager, *op. cit.*, p. 215.

[24] See, for example, Holmes' dissenting opinion in *Lochner* v. *New York* (1905).

by collective effort in the influential book, *Wealth against Commonwealth* (1894). Daniel De Leon, American Marxist and socialist leader, told an audience in 1896:

> Our system of production is in the nature of an orchestra. No one man, no one town, no one state, can be said any longer to be independent of the other; the whole people of the United States, every individual therein, is dependent and interdependent upon all the others. The nature of the machinery of production; the subdivision of labor . . . compel the establishment of a Central Directing Authority. . . .[25]

Herbert Croly provided some of the theories of Theodore Roosevelt's New Nationalism in *The Promise of American Life* (1909).

Utopian Novelists and Muckrakers

Against the sordid background, as they described it, of ruthless competition, unholy business conspiracy, the inequities of massed wealth in the hands of a few and the vast deprivation of the many, utopian novelists etched into the foreground the vision of a perfect society for America, a society ruled by brotherly love and governed by the ethics of social justice. Perhaps the most influential of these was Edward Bellamy's *Looking Backward*, published in 1888. It sold hundreds of thousands of copies in the next few years.[26] The good

---

[25] Thomas G. Manning and David M. Potter (eds.), *Government and the Economy*, rev. by E. David Cronon (New York: Holt, 1960), p. 46.

[26] Daniel Aaron, *Men of Good Hope* (New York: Oxford University Press, 1951), p. 102.

society, in his view, was one without private property, where all men served society in a kind of industrial army during the years from the age of 21 to 45, and in which power and force had given way to love and good will. There were other utopian novels in these years for the discriminate searchers after heaven on earth. William Morris provided *News from Nowhere,* and William Dean Howells wrote *A Visitor from Altruria.*

The way was prepared for utopia in the early twentieth century by writers called Muckrakers, who created a new genre of literature—the nonfiction semi-scholarly exposé. Ida Tarbell exposed the activities of John D. Rockefeller in her two-volume *History of the Standard Oil Company,* a work distinguished both for its scholarship and the righteous indignation of its author. Lincoln Steffens exposed corruption in *The Shame of the Cities.* Jacob Riis wrote sentimentally, even maudlinly, of tenement life in *How the Other Half Lives.* David Graham Phillips told of the manipulations of businessmen in government in "The Treason of the Senate." "Ray Stannard Baker investigated the railroads; in *Everybody's* Thomas W. Lawton bitterly attacked contemporary financiers; Charles Edward Russel investigated the beef trust and Judge Ben Lindsey existing abuses in criminal law . . . ,"[27] as magazines picked up mass circulation by publishing these popular exposés.

A related phenomenon was the muckraking novel, which may have had an even greater influence in conveying a picture of an American desperately in need of change and reform. There was Upton Sinclair's *The*

[27] Alfred Kazin, *On Native Grounds* (New York: Doubleday Anchor, 1956), p. 81.

Jungle, Theodore Dreiser's *Sister Carrie,* Frank Norris's *The Octopus,* Robert Herrick's *The Web of Life,* and Jack London's *The Iron Heel.*

So effectively did muckrakers mingle fact and fiction, reporting and righteous indignation, open description with covert prescription that the historian who would disentangle the reality of these years from the myth has a formidable undertaking.

There were movements, too, which took up the cudgels for collectivism and helped to spread these ideas. Prominent among these was the Social Gospel movement. Religion, which had long offered the most profound bases for individual liberty, was substantially changed as a result of this movement. Out of moral conviction, out of concern for social and economic conditions, under the influence of the theories of evolution and the sociological findings of the effect of environment upon men, preachers and thinkers formed their thought and started the movement.

Instead of being individualistic, this movement was sparked by men who conceived of society as an organism.[28] The life of an individual, they held, is inextricably bound up within this organic unity. For this reason, individual salvation is inadequate. Almost all sin involves not only the sinner but others as well, and it is pointless, in this view, to attempt to deal with it as though it were an individual matter.[29]

---

[28] Charles H. Hopkins, *The Rise of the Social Gospel in American Protestantism* (New Haven: Yale University Press, 1940), p. 125.

[29] See Walter Rauschenbusch, *A Theology for the Social Gospel* (New York: Macmillan, 1917), pp. 5-6, 20, 35-37.

Furthermore, some thought, man sins frequently
merely by participating in the social order, a participation which he can hardly avoid. Suppose, said George D.
Herron, who went from social Christianity to Christian
socialism, that one had to take a trip (in 1899), the
only practicable means of traveling would be by train.
But in traveling by train one would be involved in all
of the evils which had gone into the making of the railroads, maintaining them, and operating trains upon
them. Herron's words convey the fervor of his conviction about the evil involved in participating in society's
corruption:

> The economic system denies the right of the sin-
> cerest and most sympathetic to keep their hands out
> of the blood of their brothers. We may not go to our
> rest at night, or waken to our work in the morning,
> without bearing the burden of the communal guilt;
> without being ourselves creators and cause of the
> wrongs we seek to bear away.[30]

Many preachers of the Social Gospel believed that
before individuals could be reached and helped, society
itself must be changed. Besides their organic view of
society, these men believed in the immanence of God,
and that the Kingdom of Heaven was to be realized upon
earth. The regeneration of society was to be the first
step in the realization of this Kingdom. In what
amounted to a plan for the redemption of society, the
church had three functions, according to one theoreti-
cian: to present and embody a social ideal, to initiate
agencies and movements for the realization of the ideal,

---

[30] George D. Herron, *Between Caesar and Jesus* (New
York: Thomas Y. Crowell, 1899), pp. 24-25.

and to supply the sacrificial service necessary for the accomplishment of the mission.[31]

This plan of action did not involve, for most of the men, the prospect of violent revolution; they rather hoped to change society by convincing men of the need for reform along ideal lines planned with an intimate understanding of the workings of society. It was, in a sense, the application of some ethical ideas drawn from Christian doctrines to reform Darwinism. The full story of the impact of the Social Gospel would have to be told in terms of the work of the social action committees of many denominations, of the formation of national and international bodies to spread the ideas, and of the innumerable sermons preached to thousands of congregations embracing the Social Gospel under such church bulletin titles as "Am I My Brother's Keeper?" In this manner did collectivistic thought enter many of the churches.

Political Movements

Socialism, both in a broad and in a narrow sense, provided the ideas for political movements which made some impact upon American thought. The Socialist Labor party was organized in 1877, and ran its first presidential candidate in 1892. The party continued to grow and despite a split in its ranks, the main wing gained national following. From 1901 to 1912 the Socialist party in America grew rapidly in membership and became for a time an important factor in presiden-

---

[31] Hopkins, *op. cit.*, pp. 137-38.

tial elections.[32] More important, however, than the immediate following which the party had was the widespread dissemination of its ideas.

Socialism was based upon the view that society is an organism in the process of development. This growing organism develops according to laws differing from but analogous to the growth of the individual. Since to him the well-being of all is more important than that of any individual, the socialist believes "that the individual should subordinate himself to society, maintaining that thus alone can the welfare of all be secured. . . ."[33] Socialism is "a principle which regulates social and economic life according to the needs of society as a whole. . . ."[34] In its narrower and more precise meaning, socialism is the idea that the economy must be reorganized; private property must be abolished so far as it is a significant instrument of production; productive property must be collectively owned and managed; distribution must be carried out according to a plan based upon need.[35]

Any complete story of how collectivistic ideas were propagated by groups should call attention to the activities of certain unions, to the Progressive Movement, to the Populist Movement, and to the New Deal. Nor should I neglect an account of how, in the course of time, the halls of the academy echoed the sentiments of

---

[32] Harry W. Laidler, *Social-Economic Movements* (New York: Thomas Y. Crowell, 1946), p. 588.

[33] Richard T. Ely, *Socialism* (New York: Thomas Y. Crowell, 1894), p. 3.

[34] *Ibid.*, p. 5.

[35] See "Socialism: Principles and Outlook," *Encyclopaedia Britannica*, XX (1955 edition), p. 887.

Richard T. Ely, Lester F. Ward, John Dewey, Frederick J. Turner, Walter Lippmann, Thorstein Veblen, *et al.,* as teachers and professors presented collectivistic ideas that had become embedded in the theories of sociology, the interpretation of history, the "principles" of political science, and the "certitudes" of economics. Anyone who has been through any one of the majority of American colleges and universities in the last thirty years should have some inkling of how much a part of "education" this curvature of the mind has become.

Enough has been said, however, to show clearly that the ventures in collectivism in this century have not been simply the result of a social process rooted in social circumstances. The installation of collectivistic practices followed upon the creation of a collectivist curvature of the mind. Some circumstances lent plausibility to collectivist ideas. For example, railroads that linked towns throughout the country and industries with a nationwide market may have given a semblance of credibility to such notions as national income, national problems, and national health. But it was men who developed the ideas, spread them in literature and by movements, interpreted the meaning of circumstances, and seized the opportunities to translate a curvature of the mind into a direction for a people.

6.

The Defamation of
the American Tradition

MANY OF THE DEPARTURES from the American tradition came with dramatic swiftness in this century. A Rip Van Winkle who went to sleep in 1910 and woke again in 1935 would have discovered many of his fellow citizens strangely dependent upon government, the Constitution in many ways inoperative and grumblings about such restraints as it still imposed, numerous laws of a character with which he was unfamiliar, and a tendency to venerate leaders and to belabor those who appealed to the past. Surely, he would have concluded that a revolution had taken place, or that he had awakened in the midst of a revolution. At the least, assuming that he was a perceptive man and not too circumspect in his pronouncements, he would have declared that the American tradition had been subverted.

If such a modern Rip Van Winkle had launched inquiries to discover the sources of these changes, he might not have been satisfied with the answers he received. Undoubtedly, most of those whom he contacted would have pointed out, impatiently, that conditions had changed, that there had been war and depression, that the old opportunities were no longer available. Had he insisted upon knowing what happened to American ideals, institutions, customs, and traditions, he would probably have been dismissed as an odd fellow who could not adjust to new times and new ways.

Yet my imaginary character is not too different from a good many Americans of the recent past and today. Awaking from their private concerns and indifference (sleep), they are discovering a transformed America with mounting tendencies at odds with the tradition that they had known. One of our concerns in this condition, understandably, is to find out what happened.

The most appealing—and in some ways most comfortable—explanation is that the tradition was undermined, destroyed, and replaced by alien infiltration and communist subversion. Some historians dismiss this conception cavalierly by calling it the conspiracy theory of history—implying somehow that such a notion is disreputable on the face of it. Unquestionably, there has been and is a communist conspiracy. It is demonstrable, too, that many ideas of non-American origin have been propagated here. But such explanations attribute too much effectiveness to communists and fail to account adequately for the massive help they have had from noncommunists. It glosses over, too, the really difficult task of recovering liberty and individualism, for it ignores how deeply enmeshed in thought and ways collectivism has become.

My contention is that much of the work of subverting —I use the word in the rare sense of "to undermine the principles of; corrupt"—the American tradition was

carried on by "respectable" thinkers, writers, and scholars. I attribute to them no evil motives nor covert design, for much of their work was presented openly and
argued directly. Indeed, some of those who prepared
the way for collectivism in America apparently had no
intention of nor knowledge that they were doing so. The
effect of an action, however, is not altered by the intent
of the actor.

Discredited by Scholars

Before the American tradition was replaced, it was
discredited. Odium was attached to it, and feelings were
marshaled against it. This was no easy task to accomplish. There is every reason to believe that at the beginning of this century Americans at large were firmly
attached to constitutionalism, government by law rather
than by men, individual liberty, voluntary group activity, limited government, and personal independence.

Yet, "American" became a tainted word for many
people in the course of time. Several years ago, Karl
Shapiro, writing in *The New Republic,* referred to the
"American way of life" as a "nauseating expression"
which meant to him "the material life, the worship of
the scientific mentality, and the belief that Americans
are the best people on earth." A single instance of lynching is apt to call forth denunciations of the "American"
penchant for swift and violent justice. Should a board of
censors fail to license some obscene movie, it would be
just another horrendous example of that latent Puritanism in America which has reared its ugly head once
more. If a businessman were to question spending for

foreign aid, he might find himself used as an example of that *bête noire* of the "liberals"—the selfishly acquisitive American who stems in a long line from that vulgar preacher of penuriousness, Benjamin Franklin. "Americanism" is sealed off by quotation marks from too close a contact with it by the *cognoscenti,* who might otherwise be contaminated.

Why, it is proper to ask, should an expression such as the "American way of life" be distasteful to any American? Why should "Americanism" be used to refer to the failings of some Americans? Why should we have to flinch when we encounter the word American, fearing from experience the denunciation of the "Ugly American" that will follow?

Let us admit that some individuals have used Americanism as a cover for unwise and wrongful acts on occasion. Grant, too, that Americans taken one with another have many faults. But why should the vices of Americans be that which is conveyed by "American"? Is the summary lynching of law violators more American than trial by jury? Surely, censorship is less central to our tradition than is the liberty to publish our thoughts and opinions. Voluntary choice of church membership is more certainly a part of the "American way of life" than is scientism. Constitutionalism is much more deeply American than is materialism. The Constitution-makers took great care to guard the individual against falling prey to the bent of his neighbors to force him into conformity. Charity, both individual and organizational, is as much American as is acquisitiveness. Why then, in all fairness, does "American" not call to mind virtues as well as vices?

A *Literature of Denigration*

The major reason is rather clear to me. There was a large-scale assault upon the American tradition carried out earlier in this century. Probably the most direct attack was carried on in literature—in stories and essays, but denigration appeared more subtly in philosophy, history, political science, and theology. But the point can be made by calling attention mainly to what went on in that field known technically as literature. The heyday of this defamation came in the 1920's, though some came before and after.

H. L. Mencken, the sage of Baltimore, was likely the most uninhibited of the defamers in the 1920's. He not only pointed up the vices and failings of Americans, but he identified them with the American tradition. In the fourth volume of his vigorous *Prejudices,* Mencken asks: "What, then, is the spirit of Americanism? I precipitate it conveniently into the doctrine that the way to ascertain the truth about anything . . . is to take a vote on it, and that the way to propagate that truth . . . is with a club. This doctrine . . . explains almost everything that is indubitably American, and particularly everything American that is most puzzling to men of older and less inspired cultures. . . ."

Of Puritanism, Mencken claimed, "There is only one honest impulse at the bottom of Puritanism, and that is the impulse to punish the man with a superior capacity for happiness—to bring him down to the miserable level of 'good' men, i.e., of stupid, cowardly, and chronically unhappy men." "New England," he declares, "has never shown the slightest sign of genuine enthusiasm for ideas. It began its history as a slaughterhouse of ideas, and it is today not easily distinguishable from a cold-storage plant."

Mencken expressed an undisguised contempt for those who settled America and gave it its basic culture. "What are the characters that I discern most clearly in the so-called Anglo-Saxon type of man? I may answer at once that two stick out above all others. One is the curious and apparently incurable incompetence—his congenital inability to do any difficult thing easily and well. . . . The other is his astounding susceptibility to fears and alarms—in short, his hereditary cowardice." Even free inquiry would appear to be a wholly non-American thing. "Thus the battle of ideas in the United States is largely carried on under strange flags, and even the stray natives on the side of free inquiry have to sacrifice some of their nationality when they enlist."

As for religion, "the average American is a prude and a Methodist under his skin. . . . Save in a few large cities, every American community lies under a sacerdotal despotism whose devices are disingenuous and dishonourable. . . ." The *Boobus americanus* is taught by "oafs from the farms and villages of Iowa, Kansas, Vermont, the Dakotas, and other such backward states. . . ."

Few could match Mencken in the pithiness of his language, but others shared his scorn for things American. Frederick L. Allen may have penned the classic statement of the position in his ever-popular book, *Only Yesterday,* first published in 1931. "The typical American of the old stock," he says, "had never had more than a half-hearted enthusiasm for the rights of the minority;

bred in a pioneer tradition, he had been accustomed to
set his community in order by the first means that came
to hand—a sumptuary law, a vigilance committee, or if
necessary a shotgun." Van Wyck Brooks, long-time
chieftain of literary critics, calls the "traditional drag"
of our culture "the main fact of American history"—
writing in 1922. "If our writers wither early," he said,
"if they are too generally pliant, passive, acquiescent,
anaemic, how much is this not due to the heritage of
pioneering, with its burden of isolation, nervous strain,
excessive work, and all the racial habits that these have
engendered?"

Sinclair Lewis, a champion deflater of the American
ego, contributes this description of what he considered
to be the most typical American—the businessman, a
Mr. Jones. (Although this is taken from an introduction
to *Babbitt* that was not published at the time, it is just
the sense of what was told dramatically in the novel.)
"Mr. Jones himself . . . votes the Republican ticket
straight, he hates all labor unionism, he belongs to the
Masons and the Presbyterian Church, his favorite author
is Zane Grey, and in other particulars noted in this story,
his private life seems scarce to mark him as the rough,
ready, aspiring, iconoclastic, creative, courageous inno-
vator his admirers paint him. He is a bagman. He is a
pedlar. He is a shopkeeper. He is a camp-follower. He
is a bag of aggressive wind."

George F. Nieberg almost achieved a Mencken pitch
in his description of the American in an article in *The
Forum* published in 1931. "I lean toward the heresy that
the typical American citizen is, at best, an unpleasant
go-getter, a professional back-slapper going through his

dumb-show always a bit fearful of his job, of what people will say, of his wife—and of himself. To this heresy I will add another: that it is impossible for him to live like a civilized man, as it is impossible for him to die like one." More, "his blind, unwavering faith in 'success' stories, patent medicines, political platforms, his bootlegger's word of honor, and his boss's stupidity borders upon fanatical fervor."

Robert Herrick, in 1931, said that there "have been many instances . . . of American brutality, American tyranny, American intolerance, which have reverberated around the world." Katherine F. Gerould published an article in *Harper's* in the same year, in which she associated Americanism with gangsterism, in an attempt to explain the alleged popularity of Al Capone. "It is not because Capone is different that he takes the imagination: it is because he is so gorgeously and typically American. . . . Of course he was born in this country: could anyone but a native American have adopted so whole-heartedly American principles of action? An immigrant would have taken years to assimilate our ideals; whereas Capone was born to them. . . . There are analogies for Al Capone among the American immortals."

Writers left hardly an aspect of American behavior undenounced. In a volume of diatribes on American life published as *Civilization in the United States*, Elsie Clews Parsons attacks our sex mores. She claimed that "the lack of warmth in personal intercourse which makes alike for American bad manners and, in the more intellectual circles, for cheerlessness and aridity is due . . . to failure of one kind or another in sex relations." This failure she ascribes to the "confusion be-

tween parenthood and mating," which she says the
French handle admirably. It should be pointed out that
these critics frequently compared Americans unfavor-
ably with Europeans.

In 1931 a book called *Behold America* was published
containing the most thoroughgoing assaults upon the
tradition. In this book, most of the essays were obviously
animated by a socialist or communist ideology. I cite
them as extremes of what was a general tendency of
defamation. One writer says, "The United States is not
peaceful: its very geographic existence and its expansion in temperate North America is the result of a consistent policy of the slaughter of weaker peoples . . . and
the expropriation of their property." V. F. Calverton declares: "Unfortunately, however—*and if there is any
single explanation of why America has had no great
writers to compare with those of Europe, this is it*—no
traditions in America have ever been very genuine or
very original, and never very long-lived. . . ."

The above are but a sample of the defamations of the
American tradition. In the article alluded to earlier by
Karl Shapiro he inadvertently gives part of the explanation of why the "American way of life" should be a
"nauseating" expression to him. Calling up the names of
the major American poets of the twentieth century,
Shapiro points up how they were "anti-American-way-of-
life." Of T. S. Eliot, he says: "His entire literary output
constitutes a condemnation of American materialism,
economic greed, and cultural vacuity." Ezra Pound "is
the most scurrilous critic of American life in the twentieth century." Edgar Lee Masters "laments the corruption of pioneer stock and the hypocrisy of small-town

American life." Robinson Jeffers is described as "chief of the self-avowed enemies of American society and civilization. His attacks on American materialism and the American savagery of character have become synonymous with his poetry." The list is longer, but the point emerges: American poets heaped abuse on their country.

As to the major novelists of the 1920's, Henry S. Canby calls attention to the "dogged discontent of Ernest Hemingway, the mystic morbid discontent of William Faulkner, the strong lyric discontent of Willa Cather, the sharp scoffing discontent of Sinclair Lewis. . . ." He points out that he could easily extend the characterizations to the major dramatists. But we are all too aware of the continued vulture-like dissecting of America that still goes on among popular dramatists.

If destruction of belief in the American tradition was their aim, writers had done their work well. They had portrayed the tradition as one of narrow-minded Puritanism, of low caste Anglo-Saxons, of intolerant busybodies, of rural oafs and hayseeds, and of vulgar democrats. Whatever was good and worth while must surely have been sneaked in somehow from foreign lands. Nothing properly denotable as the American tradition could be worth preserving or even examining.

Objectives and Accomplishments

Judging from what they said, these writers were moved to this denigration by diverse aims. Some of them were unhappy about the unenthusiastic reception accorded to artists and the arts in America. Others wanted to awaken their countrymen to a more sensitive appreciation of "higher things." Socialists and communists were undoubtedly trying to arouse social-consciousness and prepare the ground for their ideas. Besides, it has been fashionable in literary circles for some time now to discover decay and disorder everywhere, and to describe it in lurid detail.

The importance of this defamation lies, however, not in the motives of those who did it but in its general impact upon Americans. H. L. Mencken, for instance, had no other national loyalty than to America, if he had that. In his mellower moods he expressed admiration for the Constitution and the Founding Fathers. But bread cast upon the waters may return in strange ways, for once the tradition had been undermined the reason for which it had been done could become separated from it. Once a writer's words are published he loses control over the uses to which they may be put.

Nor was it their numbers that gave these literary denigrators so much import. Their importance stems rather from the role of writers in modern society. Literature is the vehicle for public memories, the means by which ideas are usually spread, the device by which many creative men present their visions, the source of many of our mental images and conceptions. One may go to a play only to be entertained, but carry away with him a residue of notions which the author has implanted in his drama. "Smart" people imitate the proclaimed leaders; those who would profess to be "in-the-know" spread the ideas.

Literature can be, and often is, the means for the expression of the noblest ideas men have held, the vehicle for preserving and continuing the heritage of a people, the source of the epigrams by which people carry with them their stout beliefs. But it may also be used to undermine the tradition, to defame the heritage, to erode away the faith of a people, and to blacken the reputations of those who would uphold them. Many who were reckoned to be great writers performed this destructive task in the 1920's. The rust of their doubt entered into the iron of our tradition and continued to weaken and immobilize it long after the writers modified their assault.[1]

Fully to appreciate the sweep of the assault it must be viewed as coupled with a much more subtle and broader attack. Philosophers such as William James and John Dewey worked to undermine the belief in a fixed reality. As they succeeded, the belief in natural law which had been at the heart of the American tradition crumbled. Frederick Jackson Turner, the historian, emphasized the changing and pragmatic character of American historical development. J. Allen Smith and Charles A. Beard took positions which helped to discredit the American Constitution. Biographers "debunked" men who had been heroes to earlier Americans. Justices Oliver Wendell Holmes and Louis D. Brandeis emphasized the evolutionary character of law and the importance of changing conditions.

---

[1] It should be made clear that all criticism is not of this character. "Constructive" criticism—that which criticizes practices which fall short of the ideal—can have a salutary effect in preserving a tradition. But the criticism to which I have called attention was destructive—undermining the traditions and ideals themselves.

A Critical Period

The climax of the defamation of the American tradition—coming as it did in the 1920's and early 1930's—could hardly have been timed to achieve greater effect. It just preceded a convulsive and revolutionary period in world history. The United States—and much of the rest of the world—was hit at about this time with a lengthy and debilitating depression, and was shortly plunged into the international disorder of the late 1930's and 1940's. In other words, it was a time of trial and of searching for something firm amidst swift and unexpected change.

Traditions could have cushioned our fall and buoyed us up in crisis. They might have steadied and reassured us when trouble came. Herbert Hoover tried, for example, to direct Americans to the faith of their fathers, to the virtues of individual initiative, to the morality of private charity, but his dress reminded one of the despised Puritan, he talked too much the "hypocritical" language of rugged individualism and exuded the odor of the discredited businessman and materialism. Casting about for a faith in their time of troubles, Americans were loathe to take up a soiled tradition.

They found a faith, however, faith in men rather than law, faith in government rather than personal independence, faith in groups and collectives rather than the resolute individual. This was no accident, and the full import of the defamation is revealed in what was substituted for the American tradition. Reformers had for many years been spreading their ideas about "positive" governmental action, about the need for leaders, about the necessity for governmental action. They may have made little impact during most of the 1920's, but their efforts were intensified once the depression came, reviving hope for the acceptance of their ideas. The following titles published in the crucial years just before 1933 suggest the tenor of this material: Charles A. Beard, "The Rationality of Planned Economy," *America Faces the Future*, published in 1932; Rexford G. Tugwell, "The Principle of Planning and the Institution of Laissez-Faire," *American Economic Review*, March 1932; Stuart Chase, *A New Deal*, 1932; J. A. Hobson, *Poverty in Plenty*, 1931; Chester Davis, "Toward Planned Harvests," *Review of Reviews*, 1933; H. L. Hopkins, "The War on Distress," *Today*, 1933; and many others.

Fellow Travelers

Back of the above material lies another phenomenon of considerable moment. At the very time that the American tradition was being shattered by defamers, American travelers were giving glowing reports of another kind of society. In a recent issue (Summer 1962) of *American Quarterly*—a scholarly publication with no apparent axes to grind—Lewis S. Feuer tells of "American Travelers to the Soviet Union 1917-32: The Formation of a Component of New Deal Ideology."

By 1932, according to Feuer, the leaders in pragmatic thought had come "to regard the Soviet Union as a model of the experimental method in social practice. The whole conception of a 'social experiment,' the whole notion of planned human intervention into social processes to raise the welfare of the people, had become linked in the minds of America's intellectual and social

leaders with the practice of the Soviet Union." This link-
age he ascribes to the "work of a small number of several hundreds of travelers to the Soviet Union during
the previous decade." Among those so enthralled were
Rexford G. Tugwell, Paul Douglas, Stuart Chase, Jane
Addams, Robert M. LaFollette, W. E. B. DuBois, and
Sidney Hillman, among others. Mr. Feuer supports his
statements with references to the published writings of
these "travelers," along with illuminating quotations.

Some of the processes of social change in this century emerge from the above facts and generalizations.
The defamation of the American tradition preceded and
prepared the way for the abandonment of much of that
tradition. The subversion of American ways was not so
much the work of some secret conspiracy as it was the
result of open assaults. Whatever the intention of denigrators, they had set the stage for reformers who wished
to change the character of American society. Many of
the changes came swiftly—as in the "Hundred Days"
of the New Deal, but they were made possible by years
of work preceding them. It has not been uncommon to
interpret the departure from the American tradition in
the 1930's as a consequence of its failure in its hour of
trial. Yet in view of the above evidence, we may doubt
whether the established American ways were tried very
vigorously or shunted aside as already discredited.

7.

The Road to Collectivism

AMERICANS CAME upon the road to collectivism by diverse ways and from many paths. The signs that pointed toward this broad road filled seeker's hearts with hope by such disarming labels as "General Welfare," "Social Justice," "Economic Security," and "Freedom from Want." Some came in large groups which had been organized to advance special interests, while others came as individual stragglers. There were those drawn from the path of liberty by the siren song of utopian reformers. Tenderhearted men turned toward collectivism in the belief that it offered the best hope of alleviating the suffering which they saw or read about. The obstacles in the path of liberty— the difficulties in the way of achieving economic independence, the hardships of the individual route to personal fulfillment—convinced many of the "necessity" for joint effort. Budding intellectuals discovered a new faith in the organic conception of society, and the unsuccessful could excuse their failures as the fault of society. The destitute succumbed easily to the explanation that they were victims of oppression. Some men may be honestly convinced that they know what is best for all of us; at any rate, collectivism offered a mode

for reformers and planners—men caught in the grip of
a compelling vision—to use government to embody their
ideas in law and practice. By these and other paths did
Americans gather upon the road to collectivism.

Historically, however, the shift to collectivism was
made in the following manner. Men organized themselves in interest groups for the pursuit of common
goals. They included such groupings as farmer alliances,
labor unions, business associations, and professional organizations. These organizations frequently sought privileged status at law, and to bring the force of government to bear upon Americans to make them accede to
their demands. When they succeeded, they contested
with one another for superior position, and preyed upon
both unorganized individuals and other groups as well.
This neofeudal system (strangely enough, many "liberals" called it *progress* where labor unions were concerned) created a situation rife for the United States
government to step in and "adjust" these demands in the
public interest. This last is the face that collectivism
presents in our day.

So stated, the development appears logical and "inevitable." Is there anything strange or irregular about
men grouping together to advance common interests?
What could be more appropriate than the harmonization
of conflicting interests by action of the national government? Is not a part of American freedom the freedom
of men to associate for common ends? Was not the
republican government of these United States erected
to resolve the conflicts among contending parties and
to "promote the general welfare"? In short, have we not
come to collectivism by a logical extension of the very

ideas which informed the Constitution and have for all its days been a part of the American tradition? Or, did we reach collectivism by evading the Constitution and a profound departure from the American tradition?

These questions are of such moment for everyone— not just for historians—that they must be answered very carefully. Let us search out in our history those transitional movements from individualism to collectivism. By uncovering them, we should be able to decide how we came to this pass within a proclaimed framework of constitutionalism and a never-announced departure from liberty. What was done to effect the change is important, if the information is to be useful in finding our way back to liberty.

The mere existence of groups and organizations in a society is no indication that collectivism prevails. Alexis de Tocqueville noted in the first half of the nineteenth century that Americans were prone to the formation of all sorts of groups. Freedom to associate for common purposes *is* a basic freedom which to prohibit would be to circumscribe severely the liberty of the individual. The social and charitable functions of such groups can and have ameliorated the severities of individual responsibility and helped the individual to undertake what he could not do alone.

Resort to Coercion

Associations become a matter of public concern primarily when they use force or coercion in pursuit of their ends. So long as the individual can join and quit a group voluntarily, so long as the group is inhibited (by law and fear of punishment) from forcing its way upon others, no great harm need result from its existence. In practice, when groups have no special exemptions or privileges in law and cannot use the powers of government to force others to yield to them, individual liberty can prevail regardless of the number and variety of groups in our midst.

By turning these last two points around, it is possible to see what collectivism is. It is the institution of group force to attain the goals of groups within a society. That this is usually done in the name of society should not mislead us, for where men are free there will be conflicts as to goals, and no man's interests are fully merged with that of society. It can be shown, of course, that every man should be interested in protection from the use of force upon him, but beyond that men will have interests and interpretations quite divergent from one another. For these reasons, collectivism must always be nothing more than forcing the interests of some upon all. The thrust of collectivism is to merge all men into a common mass. For it is only by ignoring or lopping off all that is unique in the individual and dealing with that which is common to all men that collectivism can be justified.

The difference between a collectivistic society and an individualistic one can be succinctly stated. Where individual liberty is the goal, the government will exist, in considerable part, to *disarm* collectives. In a collectivist society, government will act to *empower* groups. The shift for America, then, came at those points when governments ceased to disarm groups effectively and began to empower them.

To Disarm Collectives

That the Constitution of these United States was designed to disarm collectives and prevent them from using the power of government to work their ends is attested to by no less an authority than the Father of the Constitution, James Madison. This is the burden of his argument in the justly famous "Federalist" Number 10. The problem, as he defined it, had been to erect a government that would have a "tendency to break and control the violence of faction." He explained further, "By a faction I understand a number of citizens, whether amounting to a majority or minority of the whole, who are united and actuated by some common impulse of passion, or of interest, adverse to the rights of other citizens, or to the permanent and aggregate interests of the community." It is well to note, too, that the question of whether a majority or minority wanted the action interested him only as it affected the likelihood of its enactment. Madison believed that the danger to liberty and the general welfare lay in the factional use of government for partisan ends.

He went on to explore the possibilities of preventing the partisan use of government. It could be estopped by taking away the liberty which gives rise to factions or "by giving to every citizen the same opinions, the same passions, and interests." Both of these alternatives are rejected: the first because it is undesirable and the second because it is impractical. The problem then becomes one of preventing the effects rather than removing the causes of faction. Madison held that republican government—by which he meant representative gov-

ernment—would be the one most likely to bring to
nought the effects of faction. Specifically, he maintained that the Constitution as drawn would provide
such a government. By spreading representation over
large constituencies, by having the houses of Congress
chosen in a different manner, he thought it would be
difficult for any collection of men to attain its end. The
separation of powers would add to the difficulties of
groups seeking special privileges and partisan goals. It
should be pointed out, though, that developments in
communication and transportation since Madison's day
have swept away much of the importance of the vast-
ness of the country in deterring concerted action by
groups.

The point, however, is that the purpose of the Constitution was to disarm rather than empower collectives.
Madison saw clearly that the great danger of popular
government was its susceptibility to use for partisan
ends. He desired a government which could maintain
the needed unity for external defense and internal accord but which would be inhibited by its organization
from taking precipitate and arbitrary actions that would
intrude upon the liberties of individuals. This wish he
shared with many of those who did and many who did
not approve the Constitution as drawn in 1787.

Let us follow Madison's reasoning that it is not the
existence of factions (or collectives) which really en-
dangers liberty but their gaining sway. It is not, for example, the presence of lobbyists that corrupts legislatures but the bowing of legislators to their will. Churches
limit individual liberty when they can use the powers of
the state to enact their morals or enforce their goals on

society. Business associations and corporations delimit liberty when they bring government to bear in securing special privileges. Labor unions endanger both public interest and individual liberty when they use coercion with the connivance and support of government.

That Americans have largely left off thinking in terms of individual liberty and gone over to collectivism is mirrored in current language. One hears and reads regularly of minority rights, majority rights, the rights of organized labor, the rights of business, the rights of children, the rights of women, the rights of the farmer, the rights of the people (considered collectively), and even of the rights of governments.

Common Rights, or Special Privileges?

When President Kennedy brought the influence and indirect coercive power of government to bear upon steel companies to induce them to forfeit an announced raise in prices, many of those who objected did so on the grounds that it was an attack on "business." But this is a tacit acknowledgment that "business" has special rights and privileges. From an individualist point of view, the President was either attacking the rights of all Americans, or he was threatening the rights of no Americans. The real principle involved in the steel affair (so far as individual liberty was concerned) was whether or not individuals and voluntary associations of men may act, without force, to raise or lower prices. In short, are men free to offer goods and services at whatever price they see fit, or are prices to be determined by executive fiat? The matter of monopolies and price fixing in an industry is important to liberty, but it was clearly not the issue here. *The President wanted to fix the price in the name of the public interest.* If he succeeds in this aim, he will have achieved a greater restriction upon liberty than any monopoly could without the force of government, for he acts with the force of government.

What we have, in our situation, is that government, having recognized and empowered various group interests, then tries to harmonize them. It can only do so at the expense of the liberty of all individuals, though some may believe themselves more than adequately compensated for their loss by the greater power they have at their disposal. The historical task is to point up those events and developments which marked turning points from individualism to collectivism.

There has hardly been a time in the history of these United States when contending factions were not prominent. Manufacturers early sought a protective tariff. Veterans of the Revolutionary War pressed for special privileges. Land speculators and farmers contended for different systems of dividing and pricing public lands for sale. Representatives from the East sought to hamper the westward movement, while Southerners and Westerners sought to use the federal government to acquire more and more lands to the west. Even the most careful efforts of writers of the Constitution had not managed to design a government that could not on occasion be used for partisan purposes. Indeed, the Constitution-makers yielded to faction in permitting the counting of a proportion of slaves for determining congressional representation. The Whiskey Tax was almost certainly legislation aimed to penalize a particular group—the small entrepreneurs of the back country. The Bank of the United States, as set up, may have forwarded special interests. Certainly, the protective tariffs enacted periodically from 1816 on provided special privileges for manufacturers and were disadvantageous to some shippers.

Much as one may deplore these successes of groups and factions, however, they do not indicate that America was from the beginning collectivistic. To think that they do is to confuse aberrations with central tendencies. For however much Congress, the President, or the courts might have yielded to special interests on occasion, they had not yet formally acknowledged their existence. Jefferson may have been moved by agrarian sentiments to acquire Louisiana, but it was not officially done for "agriculture." Perhaps Daniel Webster had questionable relations with "business," but he spoke for the unity of America.

Government Recognition of Factions

The turning point from individualism toward collectivism should be located at the time when formal recognition was given to groups, when the federal government began to act in the name of factions, and when the constitutional inhibitions against such actions began to break down. Until that point we are dealing with suspicions of motives rather than definite effects.

Several events occurred in the 1880's which suggest that the turn should be located thereabouts. In 1886 the Supreme Court decided, in the *Santa Clara Co.* case, that a corporation was a "person" in the meaning of the Fourteenth Amendment. By so doing it gave special status to one kind of association—the corporation. Congress made an equally substantial break with the past by the passing of the Interstate Commerce Act in 1887. Legislation aimed at any particular group is dangerous to liberty,[1] but this act had even more direct import. It provided for an Interstate Commerce Commission. As one history describes it, "The Interstate Commerce Commission was the first permanent federal administrative board to which Congress delegated broad powers of a quasi-legislative, quasi-executive, and quasi-judicial nature. Its establishment was a landmark in American constitutional history. . . . The Commission . . . represented a fundamental departure from the principle of the separation of powers."[2] Through the years other such bodies were added—Federal Trade Commission, Federal Communications Commission, Securities and Exchange Commission, National Labor Relations Board —which had the cumulative effect of bringing to nought the means set up in the Constitution for disarming groups.

Another signal departure came in 1889 with the rais-

---

[1] Government by law rather than by men requires that laws be of general applicability. As F. A. Hayek says, "Law in its ideal form might be described as a 'once-and-for-all' command that is directed to unknown people and that is abstracted from all particular circumstances of time and place and refers only to such conditions as may occur anywhere and at any time." *The Constitution of Liberty* (Chicago: University of Chicago Press, 1960), pp. 149-50.

[2] Alfred H. Kelly and Winfred A. Harbison, *The American Constitution: Its Origin and Development* (New York: Norton, 1955), p. 549.

ing of the Department of Agriculture to cabinet rank. This was the first such recognition of group or class interests by the central government, but not the last. Predictably, of course, other factions vied for similar recognition. A Department of Commerce and Labor was created in 1903, and separate departments for each were set up in 1913. Within a three-year period—1886 to 1889—the break with the tradition had been made in the legislative, judicial, and executive branches of our government.

But the way was prepared beforehand for the break. The rise of the Republican party just before the Civil War was a landmark of sectionalism, for it was the first party with so exclusively a sectional following to gain the Presidency. Its successful organization spurred the formation of even more factional parties in the South. The short-lived Freedmen's Bureau, set up toward the end of the Civil War, was a special agency of the federal government to look after the freed Negro. The Fifteenth Amendment to the Constitution—forbidding the exclusion from voting privileges on the grounds of race, color, or previous condition of servitude—adopted in 1870, may have given credence to the budding notion that there are minority rights. It was obviously intended to enfranchise a minority.

Labor Unions and Farm Groups

National groupings according to economic interests made their appearance in the latter part of the nineteenth century. It should be kept in mind, however, that it was not the existence of these organizations that ef-

fected collectivism but their empowerment by government. Accompanying the spread of large businesses
operating throughout the United States was the organization of nationwide labor unions. The National Labor
Union was organized in 1866, but expired a few years
later. Much more important and influential was the
Knights of Labor which was organized in the 1870's.
The first strike on anything like a national scale was
the Railway Strike of 1877. The American Federation
of Labor was organized in 1886 under the leadership of
Samuel Gompers. Farmers, too, turned to organization
as a means of effecting their ends. The Patrons of Husbandry (or National Grange) was founded in 1867, and
shortly began sponsoring regulatory laws. Businessmen
formed the National Association of Manufacturers in
1895. The American Anti-Boycott Association (1902)
and the Citizens Industrial Association (1903) came
into being to counter certain kinds of union activity.[3]

The increase and growth of corporations needs mention also. By 1900 two-thirds of all manufacturing in
the United States was carried on by corporations. Incorporation confers a special privilege—that of limited
liability. In return for this privileged status, corporations have long been reckoned to have a public character and to be subject to public limitations on their
activities. However, in the latter part of the nineteenth
century, due mainly to the fortuities of our federal system of government, many corporations managed to hold
their privileged status and avoid onerous limitations.
Corporate charters could be obtained in a single state,

---

[3] George E. Mowry, *The Era of Theodore Roosevelt* (New
York: Harper, 1958), p. 12.

but the resulting corporation could operate in all states. Some states—notably New Jersey and Delaware—provided unusually generous terms of incorporation. When this condition was coupled with court treatment of corporations as persons, corporations were extremely difficult to reach by regular lawful means. The resulting confusion of individual liberty with corporate "liberty" has not yet been disentangled. It created a situation ripe for governmental limitation of individual liberty in order to control corporate activity. It gave impetus, too, to the setting up of arbitrary commissions to deal with business activity.[4]

Political Parties for Special Groups

New political parties in the latter part of the nineteenth century definitely appealed to economic interest groups. There was the Greenback Labor party (organized 1878), the People's party of the U. S. A. (Populist party, organized 1891), and the Socialist Labor party (organized 1877 but only achieved national importance in the 1890's). Those historians who attribute this rise of third parties to a feeling among farmers and laborers that their interests were not being looked after by the major parties may be right. Certainly protective tariffs, land grants and subsidies to railroads, and monetary policies frequently provided advantages for financiers

---

[4] This is no attack on the corporation. I am trying to make clear that there is a valid and valuable distinction between individual and corporate activity. When this distinction is restored, it will make possible both the extension of individual liberty and regular lawful means of limiting the scope of corporate activity.

and industrial entrepreneurs. But the important point is that factions organized themselves to secure political action in their favor. They had only a limited success in the nineteenth century, however.

The progressive movement of the early twentieth century occupies an anomalous position in the march of Americans toward collectivism. This is so mainly because people of many different persuasions—socialists, nationalists, welfare staters, and free traders—adopted the rubric or have been called progressives by historians. In their stated aims, Woodrow Wilson and Eugene Debs (the candidate of the Socialist party) in 1912 were almost as far apart as it would be possible to get. Yet they are both treated under progressivism because they were reformers. The confusion is compounded because all shades of reformers did generally accept the organic conception of society. They all wanted to use the United States government to achieve positive social ends. Moreover, the idea of progress and the belief in successive stages of the development of society permeated reform thought. For these reasons, it may be that those historians who have lumped reformers together are nearer the truth than those who have made rigorous distinctions among them.

Progressive legislation does indicate that collectivism was making headway. The scope and authority of the Interstate Commerce Commission was broadened by several acts. The Pure Food and Drug Act and the Meat Inspection Act, both of 1906, show the federal government entering the arena of protecting the consumer. The Mann Act of 1910—prohibiting the interstate transportation of women for immoral purposes—extends the principle to the protection of people from themselves. Here was a clear limitation upon liberty which deals neither with the use of coercion nor even the performance of an immoral act. It deals with motives and restricts transportation. It is class legislation in that presumably men can be transported across state lines for immoral purposes without fear of penalty.

It is true that Woodrow Wilson, in 1912, proclaimed the New Freedom and declared it to be his aim to restore liberty by breaking up the trusts and removing special privileges. Yet once in office he approved the Clayton Antitrust Act which exempted labor from its provisions and provided the opening wedge for the creation of a privileged status for organized labor. The Underwood Tariff Act did free trade to some extent, but the Federal Trade Commission and Federal Reserve Board—whatever their purposes—were agencies beyond the separation-of-powers principle. The Adamson Act provided for an eight-hour day and time-and-a-half for overtime on interstate railroads, an undeniable use of government power for a faction.

Changes During World War I

Once the United States entered World War I, Wilson swiftly abandoned such relics of the New Freedom as he had held on to and turned to what might more aptly be styled the New Tyranny. The government turned from attempting to enforce competition to the co-ordination of the economy. Boards and commissions were created to deal with the various economic interests—War Industry Board, War Labor Board, Food Commission, and so forth. The Presidency supported the direct use of propaganda by way of the Committee on Public Information. The Sedition Act of 1918 restricted liberties in a manner that had not been done since the days of John Adams. The railroads were taken over and run by the government.[5]

The constitutional amendments adopted under the impetus of progressivism provided some of the legal foundations for collective action. The Sixteenth Amendment (income tax) paved the way for a redistribution of wealth and for tax policies that could be (and have been) used for the advancement of class interests. The Seventeenth Amendment (direct election of Senators) altered the republican character of the government somewhat and may have weakened the inhibitory powers which Senators would exercise on legislation. The Eighteenth Amendment (prohibition) empowered the Congress to legislate in matters of morals and to send out federal agents over the land to inquire into the activities of Americans. The Nineteenth Amendment (woman's suffrage) gave color, though not substance, to the notion that groups have rights.

The reaction to restrictive action by government was hardy and vigorous, though frequently misdirected, in the 1920's. Railroads were returned to private ownership, but the act that returned them empowered the Interstate Commerce Commission to foster mergers. The

---

[5] There are two very good reasons why I do not take up the question of whether or not these actions were "necessary" for the war effort. In the first place, I don't know— nor do all those historians who say that it was. In the second place, necessity does not alter the effects of actions, which is my concern.

Tariff Act of 1922 not only raised rates—protecting American industries as well as making it virtually impossible for European countries to pay debts—but also it carried a provision against the importation of obscene books, a provision which was sometimes interpreted to exclude works now recognized as classics. Founders of patriotic organizations were probably right in believing there were threats to Americanism, but their indiscriminate activities were hardly calculated to preserve it. Communists were driven underground by the Palmer raids, but constitutional liberties were ignored in the effort. So confused had the American tradition become that many writers and artists attributed violations of civil liberties to an American tradition of mob rule and lynch law.

Roosevelt's Hundred Days

The culmination of the trend toward the empowering of groups came with dramatic swiftness. In the "Hundred Days" following his inauguration in 1933, Franklin D. Roosevelt pushed through Congress bills which presented the country with collectivism as a *fait accompli*. All the steps toward it thus far had been but background and prelude. The central pieces of legislation were the Agricultural Adjustment Act and the National Industrial Recovery Act. By the Agricultural Adjustment Act Congress acknowledged itself as caretaker of the needs of farmers, and proceeded to provide for them by regulation, subsidies, and parity payments. Industries were invited to control themselves by fair trade codes under the NIRA. Labor was provided for by the section of the

Act which guaranteed labor's right "to organize and bargain collectively through representatives of their own choosing." A National Labor Board was created to enforce this provision. These actions marked a climax of the empowering of factions, and their aim has been fully pointed out by Rexford G. Tugwell, one of the architects of these acts. "NRA could have been administered so that a great collectivism might gradually have come out of it, so that all the enormous American energies might have been disciplined and channeled into one national effort to establish a secure basis for well-being."[6]

Although the surge into collectivism came with almost lightning quickness, the way had been prepared for it. The Depression offered the occasion, but it was not the efficient cause. For over fifty years the numbers of dependent farmers and workers had been increasing. The impotence of the individual was accentuated by the increase in size and complexity of institutions and organizations in America. A new ethos—the collectivist curvature of the mind—provided the mental bent for collective action. Actions taken during World War I provided the pattern for governmental action. The voluntary trade associations of the twenties made NRA appear to be a natural next step. Never-ending protective tariffs had accustomed Americans to collective action for particular interests. Organized labor's special status had already been recognized by the Norris-La Guardia Anti-injunction Act of 1932.

The NIRA and AAA were nullified by the Supreme

---

[6] Quoted in Arthur M. Schlesinger, Jr., *The Politics of Upheaval* (Boston: Houghton Mifflin, 1960), p. 214.

Court, but these decisions did not stem the tide of collectivism. Even before the courts nullified these laws, Roosevelt had launched upon a different course. Business lost much of its privileged status when NRA succumbed, and the administration cast it into that limbo in which it has usually existed since—subjected to harassment, regulation, and periodic threats of investigation and dismemberment. Meanwhile, Roosevelt and his congressional followers turned to providing protection and benefits for the "underprivileged" and "unfortunate." (The argot of the New Dealers implied that all wealth and station resulted from special privileges and good luck.) The Social Security Act was class legislation to provide benefits for wage workers. Massive relief was provided from 1935 to 1939. The National Labor Relations Act of 1935 gave organized labor increased status and included prohibitions of employer activity against unions. The Revenue Act of 1935 increased the surtax rate on individual incomes, raised rates on large corporations, and estate and gift taxes were increased. In 1937 the Farm Security Administration was set up to aid tenant farmers, and in 1938 a new Agricultural Adjustment Act was passed, reinacting the protected position of farmers.

Entrenched Interests

Over the years since, organized labor has consolidated its privileged position. Farmers have become accustomed to subsidies and crop controls. Government aid has been extended to more and more of the population by way of extension of Social Security and through

such devices as FHA loans. Many businesses became accustomed to cost-plus contracts during and after World
War II, and have managed by manipulation to acquire
privileged positions. Minimum wages and hours coupled
with wage bargaining by industry has tended to make
prices inflexible and to stifle competition. Amidst the
pulling and hauling of privileged groups for a greater
share of the "national income," the cry increases for
government to act to harmonize these interests. Some
want laws prohibiting labor unions from striking; others
want wage, price, and rent controls. Governmental action during World War II set further precedents for
control which have not yet been extended to peacetime
use. One more good emergency should provide the setting for wiping out the remaining vestiges of liberty in
America, since we have both the practice and the beliefs for it.

The road we have taken toward collectivism has now
been pointed out. It was made possible for us to come
upon this road by ignoring and evading the Constitution. Groups were empowered rather than disarmed as
they gained recognition and privileges from governments. Once this has happened, it can be made to appear that the completion of the circle is inevitable. If
farmers can use government to raise food prices, if organized labor can use force aided and abetted by government to drive up wages, if corporations can operate
with only arbitrary limitations, who is to protect the
public interest? The obvious answer is that the United
States government must act to resolve conflicts and protect the general welfare. But it is not the only answer.
If liberty be accepted once more as the goal, if govern-

ment will once again disarm groups, we can return to liberty. By marking out the trails by which we have come to collectivism, I have also uncovered the signs which we may follow to recover the path of liberty.

8.

Some Defenders of Individualism

COLLECTIVISTS did not press their cause by making a direct assault upon individual liberty. On the contrary, they frequently urged the necessity for their programs on the grounds that only by such action could individual freedom be advanced. They did, however, as I have pointed out, adopt and spread basic ideas which were antithetical to individual liberty—thus undermining the foundations. By working to discredit the beliefs in an order in the universe, in reason, in freedom of the mind and will, they disjoined liberty from responsibility and cut away the bulwarks to liberty. This was done by substituting determinism, relativism, irrationalism, and scientism for older beliefs. Pragmatism replaced the quest for Truth; materialism gained sway over idealism; utopian humanism gained ground upon the belief in a moral order. In a sense, collectivism crept in behind the smokescreen of confusion in the realm of ideas that characterized the latter part of the nineteenth century.

But all of this was most subtle. A direct attack upon individual liberty—if it had come first—could have been recognized and countered. There were, of course, socialists, anarchists, and communists who advanced their causes openly and sometimes directly, though they met with little success and stubborn resistance. The victories of the twentieth century, however, belonged not to Eugene Debs and Norman Thomas but to men like Paul Douglas and Walter Lippmann, who forsook recognizable doctrinaire positions for a pragmatic Fabianism. By so doing, they were able to advance collectivism at the weakest points of resistance to it at any given moment, riding the crest of every favorable wave of ideas. Thus it was that much liberty had been lost before there was any general awareness of what was going on.

Josiah Royce

Here and there, however, a man appeared who saw from the outset the fatal impact that the adoption of scientism, relativism, pragmatism, materialism, and irrationalism would have upon freedom and individualism. One of the earliest of these was Josiah Royce. Royce's life (1855-1916) parallels the period of the development and spread of these radical ideas, and he worked in the midst of the great controversies about them. He devoted much of his great talent to the refutation of the various virulent determinisms and to the defense of freedom and the possibility of individuality. Josiah Royce was a philosopher and a professor, a contemporary of William James on the faculty of Harvard University. But while James was establishing himself as the outstanding spokesman for pragmatism—a pseudo-philosophy which cut the ground from under all philosophy—Royce was making a valiant and subtle stand for traditional philosophy and its enduring concerns. While

James declaimed against the "tyranny" of truth, Royce clung tenaciously to the search for Truth.

Royce was an idealist, a theist, a rationalist, a revisionist Calvinist, a philosophical follower of Kant and Hegel, and one of a very small number of great American philosophers. The central philosophical problem with which he wrestled was how there can be individuality and freedom in the universe. As he put it, "The problem of Individuality . . . is the most central and important one. . . . I felt this fact, although with less clearness, from the first."[1] To put it more directly, how can there be freedom if there is a moral order in the universe? If there is an all-knowing God, how can there still be choice for individuals? If there is cause and effect operating in the world, how can men be free? If there is a final unity, how can there be diversity?

That most men today—even thinkers—could not understand these problems, much less be concerned about them, is but a measure of how far we have come from the belief in ultimate truth, the final triumph of righteousness, and the real existence of a moral order. Perhaps one day we will become aware of the importance of these great questions once more. But in the meanwhile we must pass over most of them to treat of those questions which are even at the moment live ones. They would be those bearing most directly upon the collectivist premises.

The collectivist views man as a social creature, as largely a product of his heredity and environment, as lacking significant freedom and responsibility, as living

---

[1] Josiah Royce, *The World and the Individual* (New York: Macmillan, 1923), II, xiv.

under the imperative of adjustment to the "require-
ments" of society. Scientism provides the operative mode
for prescribing the character of this required adjustment. We have all encountered this at the very practical
level. What should the sexual laws of a country be?
Make a survey of the sexual habits of the people and
find out. What should be done about the housing of a
people? Make a survey of living conditions and find out.
Where should government moneys be spent? Make a
survey of employment conditions and find out.

Royce denied the validity of the fundamental premises
upon which environmentalism, social adjustment, and
determinism are based. In the first place, Royce maintained that science does not tell us what ought to be; it
is only a means of describing what is. Scientific facts
are, themselves, void of ethical content. The world with
which science deals, "the world in space and time, the
world of causes and effects, the world of matter and of
finite mind," is only "a very subordinate part of reality."[2] His meaning is this: The important part of reality
is the realm of morality, of choice, of responsibility, of
individuality. Science deals only with those aspects of
reality which things have in common, not with uniqueness and difference. It treats only of the caused, never
of the uncaused—that is, the moral.

The theories of social adjustment got their imperative
from the belief in automatic progress that was buttressed by Darwinian evolution. According to this view
all change is progress, the latest is the best, and the
duty of man is to adjust to these changes. In the second

---

[2] Josiah Royce, *The Spirit of Modern Philosophy* (Boston:
Houghton Mifflin, 1897), p. 344.

place, then, Royce denied this doctrine of automatic change and the imperative of adjustment. He had no quarrel with the physical theories of evolution; they had as much and as little validity for him as any other data provided by the empirical sciences. It was when the social application was made to the theories of evolution that he rushed to combat them.

The fallacy, he thought, was the equating of the process of evolution with progress. The theory simply would not stand up; change is an amoral concept; progress implies a system of values by which to measure the change. If potatoes sprout in the basement, that is a part of the process of evolution; but it is not progress. An egg beginning to incubate is a part of the process of evolution, but if it was intended for table use, that could hardly be called progress. Royce declared that "the theory that founds morality wholly upon these facts of evolution is defective because it confuses the notion of progress, the conception of growth in complexity and definiteness with the conception of the growth in moral worth."[3]

In short, there is a confusion of physical development with moral growth—the latter being real progress, in Royce's view. Once this distinction is accepted, there is no reason to adjust to every change in society. To so adjust would be to become a "link in its mechanism, or a member of one of its numerous herds, in any case a mere vehicle for carrying its various influences."[4]

---

[3] Josiah Royce, *The Religious Aspect of Philosophy* (Boston: Houghton Mifflin, 1895), pp. 27-28.

[4] Josiah Royce, *The Philosophy of Loyalty* (New York: Macmillan, 1908), p. 82.

Third, Royce denied the validity of all absolute determinisms. But in so doing he tried to take into account the tremendous influence of heredity and environment. On this score, he said: "By nature I am a victim of my ancestry, a mass of world-old passions and impulses, desiring and suffering in constantly new ways as my circumstances change, and as one or another of my natural impulses comes to the front. By nature I have no personal will of my own."[5] Or again, one's conduct may be a result of what the environment does to his "hereditary predispositions" and "instinctive tendencies."[6]

By these sayings Royce appears to have yielded to the determinists. Not so, however. He is saying, rather, that by nature man is an animal, by nurture a social being. These are the scientifically observable facts. But Royce believed that man can become a free and responsible individual. His exposition of the means by which this can take place is the heart of his philosophy.

Royce affirmed the absolute necessity of freedom for the individual. In various places in his writings, he declared that individuals must be self-possessed, personally independent in judgment, free to call their souls their own, free to choose, free to act, "sufficiently independent of one another to make their freedom of action possible and finally significant."[7] It should be noted that this does not call for absolute independence of other beings, complete unrelatedness to the remainder of the universe,

---

[5] *Ibid.*, p. 31.

[6] Josiah Royce, *The Problem of Christianity* (New York: Macmillan, 1913), I, 127.

[7] Royce, *The World and the Individual*, I, 395.

nor freedom from the consequences of acts. But it is
essential for a man to have all the freedom necessary for
independent thought, action, and responsibility.

Responsible thought and action are the keys to the
whole puzzle. Royce maintained that there is a moral
order in the universe. Man's highest imperative is to
become a moral being, thus relating himself positively to
all reality. Now if the universe is moral, and if individuals participate in this morality, they must be so free
from one another and from mutual predetermination
that their acts can be described as moral. If a man's
actions are attributable finally to any other source than
himself, he is not responsible for them.

Freedom is not only necessary for individuality, but
even more significant, it is the *result* of individuality.
This is a strange and paradoxical idea to express. What
does it mean? Now it is clear that only as the individual
makes choices does he exercise his freedom. Man is not
free and thus an individual; he must become an individual by asserting his own will, by making choices, and
by acting upon them. In short, he becomes an individual as a result of the choices that he makes; as he
makes choices, he becomes free and self-determining.

But is choice possible? That is the crux of the whole
matter. Royce maintained that it is, that man is psychologically, mentally, and spiritually equipped to make
choices. Psychologically, choice is made possible by the
faculty of *attention*. It is a commonly experienced phenomenon that the mind can attend to whatever it
chooses. Royce gave the example of an idea entering
the mind of a man. The idea can be pushed aside or it
can be made the sole object of the attention. If he

fastens upon it, it may grow until it dominates and permeates the whole mind.

Man's mental ability to make choices is his capacity to reason. Reason should serve as arbiter among the objects or ideas upon which one may fix his attention. "Choice is a mental process," said Royce, "that involves the presence of plans for the satisfaction of desires, a foreknowledge of relatively objective ends that constitute the conscious aims of these desires, a more or less reasonable estimate of the value of these aims. . . ."[8] Reason plays another role in choice also. In order to fix his attention the individual must consciously intend to do so. If attention is conscious, then it is possible for the choice of attending to be made rationally. He can reflect upon and analyze the choices.

Spiritually, man needs meaning and purpose in his life. It is in the choice of these purposes, goals, or ideals that a man distinguishes himself from others. By attending to them, too, he is drawn outside himself, freed from the hereditary and environmental determination of his actions. By attaching himself to ideals he lays an enduring foundation for sturdy independence. By devotion to ideals he can achieve self-expression and fulfillment. This purpose gives individuality and integrity to the life of the individual. It is impossible, Royce thought, that the true purpose of an individual should be anything but unique. For that purpose is "to find for yourself just your own place in God's world, and to fill that place, as nobody else can fill it."[9] It gives integrity be-

---

[8] Josiah Royce, et al., The Conception of God (New York: Macmillan, 1897), p. 188.

[9] Royce, The World and the Individual, II, 294.

cause all the fragments of life and experience can be thought of in terms of that purpose, as either fulfilling it or contrary to it.

There is a great deal more to Royce's thought than this would suggest. He thought that one becomes truly an individual as he relates himself to God and His purpose. Moreover, through the fulfillment of himself the individual entered freely into social purposes. But the subtlety and remoteness of Royce's thought must not be allowed to obscure his advocacy of an everyday sort of individualism. Regarding this matter, he said: "Be an individual; seek your own individual good; seek that good thoroughly, unsparingly, with all your heart and soul."[10]

William Torrey Harris

Another man who perceived early the fatal tendencies for individualism of ideas becoming current in his day was William Torrey Harris. Harris was even more of a rationalist than Royce. Like Royce, he was a follower of Kant and Hegel, an idealist, an opponent of materialism, a writer, and somewhat of a philosopher. Harris lived at a time (1835-1909) when many of the ideas which he championed were in the ascendant. He was a New Englander by birth, a Midwesterner by adoption, and an educator by trade. He crowned an active career in education by serving as United States Commissioner of Education (1889-1905).

In general, Harris combined in his thinking both conservative and libertarian ideas. He was, perhaps, more

---

[10] Royce, *The Philosophy of Loyalty*, p. 80.

of a traditionalist than Royce. At a time when it was already coming under attack, Harris was an ardent champion of the American way of life. That "way" he identified with individualism and freedom.

The individual should be left free to manage his own affairs, Harris maintained, so long as his doings concern himself alone. The state should not go beyond providing punishment for overt violations of its laws. There is a difference between sin and crime, and only the latter is the proper concern of the state. If a deed does extend its effects beyond the individual, if it is an overt act, then the smallest governmental unit with jurisdiction over the area affected should take cognizance of and punish the offender. This, according to Harris, was the principle of local self-government in America, and he thought it should be carefully observed.

America was founded by men who wished to be as free as possible from the dictation of the social whole. The ideal of America was that each man should receive the fruits of his deeds, Harris thought, and that each man should be free to seek his own good in his own way. Negatively, government should limit itself to protecting the life, liberty, and property of the individual; positively, it should take only such measures as would help a man to help himself. Harris objected to socialism on the ground that it would not aid in making the individual self-sufficient. Granted, there were inequalities in the wealth of citizens, and there was extreme poverty in the land. Socialism proposed to solve this inequity by governmental ownership and control of production, and distribution according to need.

But what relationship did this proposed cure bear to

the cause of the disease? Very little, Harris thought; the inequities were caused by poor habits of thrift, industry, and management. Governmental aid would not encourage or produce industry, skill, frugality, and temperance in those lacking them, and might well destroy all incentive for developing those desirable traits in everyone. Socialism proposes, said Harris, "to abolish altogether the idea of thrift . . . by removing all occasion for its exercise."[11]

In giving voice to these and similar ideas, however, Harris was simply expressing an agreement with the then prevailing ethos. They have since gone out of style, but in nineteenth century literature it would be possible to find hundreds of iterations of them. It is not, then, in these ideas that the importance of Harris as a thinker is to be discovered. It is rather in his repudiation of materialism, determinism, and scientism, and his affirmation of freedom, responsibility, and individualism.

Harris rejected all varieties of determinism. He denied the ultimate validity of materialism upon which most if not all of the secular determinisms were based. The deterministic interpretation of evolution made him shudder, he declared, and he deplored such "a dreadful theory of evolution."[12]

The doctrine of force proposed by Herbert Spencer and others was repugnant to him. He declared that neither movement and change nor individuality could be explained by external force. Spencer's theories, Harris

---

[11] William T. Harris, "Statism vs. Socialism," *The Forum,* XXIV (September, 1897), 189.

[12] William T. Harris, "Is Education Possible without Freedom of the Will?" *Education,* XVI (January, 1896), 304.

thought, led to the dependence of all being, and thus removed any basis for freedom and responsibility. Indeed, he thought this was an inevitable conclusion from an exclusive reliance upon science as the means of acquiring truth. The scientific method can only be used to reach deterministic conclusions, for "the mind disciplined solely in observing dependence and external relations becomes of the opinion that it is not necessary to assume self-activity to explain anything in nature. All may be explained by outside influence."[13]

Harris was not an opponent of science so long as it remained in its subordinate role of helping to provide man with information about how to do what he wished to do; scientific thought, however, was a low stage of thought and should have nothing to say about ultimate reality. He was asked in a committee meeting on one occasion what stage the scientist had reached who constructed an atomic theory. Mr. Harris replied that "atomism is the philosophy which makes the sensible world transcendental. It is the philosophical idealization of the lowest kind of knowing."[14]

Harris objected as well to the sociological literature of his day (and would have of ours as well, no doubt), declaring that it was "a stream of demoralizing theory based on the notion that our psychological activity is a phenomenon in a stream of causation—determined by its antecedents and not modified by any action of an in-

---

[13] William T. Harris, "The Study of the Natural Sciences—Its Uses and Dangers," *Education*, X (January, 1889), 285.

[14] William T. Harris, "How the Will Combines with the Intellect in the Higher Orders of Knowing," *Journal of Proceedings and Addresses of the National Education Association*, XXXV (1896), 448.

dependent or transcendental will."[15] The notion that motives determine behavior was repugnant to him. A motive, he pointed out, represents a possibility of action,
not a determination of the course to be followed. This
may appear a slight and unimportant distinction; yet, if
it were accepted, the bulk of the literature upon which
reform has been predicated for the last hundred years
would be discredited.

Harris not only denied the validity of determinism but
also pointed out his reasons for doing so. One of his
main points was that determinism does not explain
reality as men know it. Determinism cannot account for
variety, change, originality, or individuality. Determinism admits change, and supposes it to be the result
of a totality of causative conditions. But change means
something different from what was. How can like things
produce unlike things, Harris asked? This is impossible,
he replied to his own question; a mould cannot produce
both a cube and a globe. "If things change, their change
is a proof that there was no constraining necessity in the
shape of a totality of existing conditions. There must
have been a contingency—this thing had other possibilities. . . ."[16] Further, any being which is caused from
without is a dependent being; it is not a whole but rather
a part of that upon which it is dependent. If such dependency were the case, there would be no true individuals.

This misunderstanding arises from a failure to think

[15] William T. Harris, "Herbart's Unmoral Education," *Education*, XVI (November, 1895), 180.

[16] Harris, "Is Education Possible without Freedom of the
Will?" *Education*, XVI, 303.

clearly, Harris thought. The deterministic theories of causation fail ultimately to account for anything. What the determinist has is a series of effects with no final or absolute cause. Begin with a series, say, A, B, C, D, E, etc., in which B is the effect of A; C is the effect of A and B; D is the effect of A, B, and C; E is the effect of A, B, C, and D; and so on. The questions must eventually arise concerning the cause of A.

When this question arises, an ultimate problem must be solved; there must be a cause which is itself not an effect; there must be a final cause, an independent being. This would make a First Cause necessary, but it would not make independent individuals necessary. Independent individuals are necessary, however, to account for change. If there were only a First Cause, there would be no variety and multiplicity, for everything which proceeded from the Cause would be like unto it. Free, undetermined individuals are necessary to account for the world as men know it, else change and variety are illusory.

Self-activity was the term used most often by Harris to indicate man's freedom from determination, his active rather than passive role in the world. Self-activity is a fact, Harris declared, a fact discoverable by internal observation or introspection: "Our thinking, feeling, and willing are forms of self-activity, and inconceivable without admitting it."[17] It is a fact deducible even from the activities of higher animals.

Take the case of the cause of the movement of an animal. Suppose a horse is hitched to a carriage, with a

---

[17] William T. Harris, *Psychologic Foundations of Education* (New York: Appleton, 1899), p. 112.

man in the carriage. The man hits the horse with a whip, and the horse begins to move pulling the carriage. The proximate cause of the movement of the horse and carriage is that the driver hit the horse across the back with a whip. But causation must explain more than this. Whence comes the energy which propels the carriage? No one would seriously maintain that it comes from the whip; indeed, it is obvious that the energy comes from the horse. And that energy was used because the horse willed to go rather than to be beaten.

But the above is an example of a low form of self-activity, as Harris conceived it. God is fulfilled self-activity, creativity, individuality; man is capable of and responsible for achieving self-activity. Physical action is but an outward sign of self-activity. It is the soul or the mind which is self-active in the highest sense, "a pure self-activity which makes its product . . . for the sake of self-revelation."[18] The spiritual, then, is superior to the physical. Determinism presupposes a situation where the physical is dominant, but this is a transposition of the order which should exist. In short, the determinist has reversed the order of the origin of things, and professes to see matter the moving force; whereas, in reality, spirit is the mover and matter passive. Freedom becomes much easier to perceive once reality is viewed from its proper perspective.

But, according to Harris, man is not born free. He is born a physical being and has to become a spiritual being. This, Harris thought, was the true meaning of evolution, the progress of a man toward freedom and individuality. Man must progress through three stages

---

[18] *Ibid.*, pp. 113-14.

of thought on this extended journey. The first stage is that of sense perception. At this level, each object appears to be separate from all other objects and to possess a reality of its own. This view may be described as particularistic or nominalistic. Things are not seen in their relation to one another, but rather they appear to exist apart from all relation. This is the level of common sense. "Common sense assumes that experience has before it a world of complete individual beings which either are or are not, and do not exist in a state of becoming or change, nor depend essentially upon one another."[19] This is the lowest level of thought, Harris believed, and the child must be hastened through and beyond it before he is stuck irretrievably in this groove.

The second state of thought about reality is the relational or scientific stage. On this level, all things are viewed in their relation to one another. This is the stage when men will devise theories of determinism, where everything will be viewed as caused by something else. Nothing is viewed as a whole, but rather is seen as a part or result of that which went before.

The third and highest level of thought may be denoted as pure reason or insight. This is the level, Harris explained, where men have withdrawn themselves "out of their finitude and littleness, out of their feelings and prejudices, up into the region of the pure intellect, the region of unbiased judgment, so as to survey a subject in all its bearings."[20] Here is thought concerned with

---

[19] *Ibid.*, p. 220.

[20] William T. Harris, "University and School Extension," *Journal of Proceedings and Addresses of the National Education Association*, XXX (1890), 250.

wholes, with the ultimate verities, with independence, self-activity, freedom, and individuality.

The process of reaching this freedom was described by Harris in this way: The first step in freeing the mind is the act of attention. Attention enables the mind to remember. Memory frees the mind from its spatial and temporal circumstances. Through attention the mind is able to combine experience and to think about it or analyze it. "Analysis is composed of repeated acts of attention. The will isolates the object and excludes others from it; then again it selects a portion of this object for its minuter attention, excluding the rest of the object. . . "[21] In analysis all things are viewed as separate entities. By the attending of the mind to relationships, it is able next to discover the apparent relativity of all things. This process he called synthesis, and by synthesis one arrives at a stage where all things are interconnected. To reach the last stage of knowledge—insight—the will is the most vital element. At this highest level of thought the will inhibits or forces from the attention sense perception, memory, analysis, synthesis, and reflection, leaving the mind free for pure thought. The mind can then be occupied with inquiries about "the nature of a whole or total," and can find "the categories of independence and self-activity."[22]

The way to this highest level of thought is through attention, reason, and imagination. What is discoverable at this level are ideals. By focusing upon ideals, the

---

[21] Harris, "How the Will Combines with the Intellect in the Higher Orders of Knowing," *Journal of NEA*, XXXV, 442.

[22] Harris, *Psychologic Foundations of Education*, p. 245.

individual is cut loose—freed—from the constraint from the chain of circumstantial necessity and material forces. As Harris put it, man's self-direction rests upon his power to see "beyond the real things before the senses to the ideal possibilities invisible to the brute."[23] Harris described the process in this way:

> Standing in the center of the universe with chains of causation which reach out to infinity in all directions, the ego by its intellect inhibits this progressive chain and introduces a thought of its non-being, a thought of an ideal different from its real. Then it interposes again with its will and modifies this chain of causation so as to become responsible for a new line of modifications which it has itself originated.[24]

By this innovation with and departure from the natural chain of causation, man acts freely and becomes responsible for his actions.

Neither Royce nor Harris were primarily concerned with defending individual liberty. In their day, the protections of liberty appeared secure. Harris could still visualize an era of expanding individual liberty ahead, for he lived in an age when most of the signs still pointed in that direction. The vast waves of tyranny which have swept over or now batter against the edifice of liberty were then but a gentle incoming tide, lapping at the foundations. Yet in intellectual circles the assault upon freedom—the intellectual bedrock of liberty—was already far advanced.

---

[23] William T. Harris, "Vocation vs. Culture," *Education,* XII (December, 1891), 204.

[24] Harris, "Herbart's Unmoral Education," *Education,* XVI, 181.

The Vital Difference

Freedom is a private, personal, and inner matter, by its very nature not public. On the face of it, freedom would concern deep thinkers among theologians and philosophers. After all, governments cannot create it, nor perhaps even affect it at this level. Liberty, on the other hand, is the much grosser public affair. Governments can protect it, acknowledge it, invade it, and perchance abolish it. Thus it would appear that men might devote themselves to liberty and leave individuals to shift for themselves regarding freedom.

But there is a connection between freedom and liberty. If men cease to believe in the possibility of freedom, liberty is no longer supportable as a public condition. If freedom is not possible, men are not responsible for their actions, and their liberty will have to be reduced, or, at least, there will be intellectual justification for doing so.

Long before it became apparent to most men, then, Royce and Harris detected the erosion of belief which would undercut liberty. They perceived the nature of the destructive ideas—materialism, scientism, determinism, and the doctrines of adjustment to the social whole. They affirmed the validity of freedom of the mind and will, and of the necessity of a belief in God, in an order in the universe, in reason, in ideals, and in the imagination to support these ideas.

The historical influence of these men, thus far, has probably been slight. They were near anachronisms when they were at the height of their powers, and they have been largely ignored since. Yet it is not considered good taste among American intellectuals today to avow determinism (though many of them continue to approve and advance programs based upon it), and the day may be at hand when such thinkers as Harris and Royce can help to point the way out of the intellectual dilemmas into which we have fallen.

9.

The Failure of Compromise

POLITICS, WE are told by what is now the "conventional" wisdom of political science, is the art of compromise. This is a most plausible idea. If men differ from one another about what to do, how are these differences to be resolved? The most obvious alternatives are compromise or a resort to force. Surely it would not be good for a people to resort continually to armed combat to settle their differences. It would appear, then, that compromise is the great imperative—even virtue—of statecraft.

But this doctrine of compromise is more complex than the above reasoning would suggest. Compromise suggests that both sides yield ground, that they "split the difference," as it were. In fact, however, this has seldom been the case in political matters. Let us take an example. Suppose that the country is divided into two parties over an issue—the tariff, say. One party favors free trade, and the other wants a protective tariff. The protectionists introduce a bill into Congress which provides for protective duties on certain imports. A "compromise" is worked out between the free traders and protectionists. It would involve lower rates than those originally proposed, and perhaps fewer items on the protected list. This would appear to meet the qualifications for a "compromise," but it is far from a splitting of the differences. The party of free trade has agreed not only to a quantitative compromise, but it has yielded up its principle as well. The protectionist party has begun the establishment of its principle and has, presumably, yielded ground temporarily on the amount and degree of the tariff.

In brief, compromise can be made to work entirely to the advantage of one side. It is my contention that it has usually done so in the United States in the twentieth century. This explains why it is such a prime virtue among the "liberals." For, to put it more directly, when compromises have been made, they have usually redounded to the advantage of collectivists and to a compromise of principle by individualists.

Such a state of affairs came about in this way. Many of the principles of individualism were established in America at the beginning of the twentieth century. On the other hand, collectivists were only beginning to come to the fore with their innovations. As the attack upon individualism mounted, individualists became *defenders,* and the *offensive* was seized by collectivists. When one side is proposing innovations and the other is trying to stand its ground, the innovators must gain ground by any compromise. Collectivists must realize this, for they have been advocates of compromise as a virtue. This course of development demonstrates, too, the validity of the old adage that the best defense is a good offense.

The defection of the intellectuals to, or toward, collectivism gains tremendous importance from this perspective. They are the thinkers within a society, the ones who propose solutions for problems which arise. When every new problem is presented as calling for a collectivist solution, when history and political science are written to demonstrate the "necessity" for collectivism, when the motives of individualists are presented as "selfish" and collectivists are imputed to be men of "good will," when the media of communication are filled with statements containing implicit collectivist assumptions (and this state of affairs has existed for a long while), it is not surprising that politicians should succumb to confusion and indirection. (What is surprising is that as many congressmen have held out against this trend as have, which helps to explain, incidentally, why we witness a continuing assault upon Congress.)

Intellectuals have aided the cause of a gradual movement toward collectivism via compromise and by adopting and spreading pragmatism. Pragmatism places the emphasis upon results rather than upon principles. Theoretically, this might work as well for individual liberty as for collectivism. It would if both sides were founded upon principle; that is, it would not work for either. But in fact collectivism is not founded upon principle; it is founded rather upon a vision of a utopian social condition. Thus, any means toward that end are often justified. Results are what count. In effect, then, pragmatism is used to support those compromises by which collectivism is advanced.

It follows, then, what must be pointed out: *the compromises fatal to individual liberty were made not by collectivists but by would-be individualists.* Indeed, the initial compromises were not even made under collectivist pressure. Many businessmen came to the defense of individualism in the twentieth century, and indeed they had opposed government controls and regulations in the nineteenth century. Yet it was businessmen who first acquired a privileged position in America. (I speak not of "business" as a class, for so far as I know no such class exists or has existed, but rather of some businessmen.) They were the ones who benefited most directly by protective tariffs, government subsidies and grants, and the limited-liability corporation. This set the stage for other groups to cry for like privilege, and gave color of truth to the notion that all wealth resulted from privilege.

The best example, however, of the failure of compromise for the cause of individual liberty is the administration of President Herbert Hoover. This is so for several reasons. Hoover was President in the midst of the Great Depression, a development heralded as the final test of the validity of individualism. Hoover identified himself as the spokesman for "American Individualism." He was adjudged to have failed in coping with the depression, and this has been interpreted as the failure of reliance upon individual liberty.

Hoover: the Individualist

Now there should be no doubt that in any division of men as between individualists and collectivists Hoover should be ranked with the individualists. His writings, speeches, state papers, and memoirs are eloquent evidence of that fact. In 1922 he published a book called *American Individualism;* his presidential messages are replete with references to individual liberty, and as early as 1934 he published a book, *The Challenge to Liberty,* pointing up the collectivistic tendencies of the Roosevelt administration.

Nor should it be thought that Hoover did not understand the philosophy behind individual liberty. Some references to his thought should make it clear that he did. He identified the American way with individual liberty, and said of that way:

> The American way acknowledges the Fatherhood of God, the dignity of man. It knows no rank, no caste, no exclusions. It recognizes man's right to personality, to freedom of choice, to freedom of will and judgment; the right to think, to believe, to have faith, to dream, to speak, [to] write. It insists that these inalienable freedoms of mind and spirit come from the Creator himself, not from the state. . . .[1]

Indeed, according to Hoover, government is the real enemy of freedom. It is against this enemy that the American system has stood. Hoover said, "Our structure of government, our political, social, and economic ideals and practices have, in all these centuries, been a vigilant defense against the power of the State, the power to use force, to enslave."[2]

Hoover often insisted upon the importance of economic freedom. He explained that "other freedoms cannot be maintained if economic freedom be impaired."[3]

---

[1] Herbert Hoover, *Addresses upon the American Road,* 1941-1945 (New York: D. Van Nostrand, 1946), p. 259. There are several volumes of Hoover's collected speeches. This one will be referred to hereafter as *Addresses,* IV.

[2] *Ibid.*

[3] *Ibid.,* pp. 167-68.

Men are not free unless they can "choose their jobs and callings, bargain for their own wages and salaries, save and provide by private property for their families and old age."[4] This freedom benefits all, Hoover declared, because free men will develop "a dynamic, not a static, philosophy of life. Free men generate new ideas, new inventions. From them comes change, reform, and progress."[5]

Hoover warned, too, against the futility of attempts to legislate freedom. Regarding such legislation, he said it should be tested by this question: "Does this or that act increase or protect or does it limit or destroy intellectual or spiritual freedom? Does it make for the dignity of man . . . ?"[6] He maintained that governmental activities must be confined within "certain boundaries. We must find solution to our problems without impairment of the checks and balances and their guarantees."[7] The way to accomplish this goal is for the people to "cure abuse and forward progress without the government action. That is self-government in the highest form of which democracy has yet given conception—that is self-government outside of government."[8]

---

[4] *Ibid.,* p. 222.

[5] Herbert Hoover, *Addresses upon the American Road, 1945-1948* (New York: D. Van Nostrand, 1949), p. 52. Hereafter cited as *Addresses,* V.

[6] Herbert Hoover, *Addresses upon the American Road, 1933-1938* (New York: Scribner's, 1940), p. 193. Hereafter cited as *Addresses,* I.

[7] Herbert Hoover, *The Challenge to Liberty* (New York: Scribner's, 1934), p. 145.

[8] Herbert Hoover, *State Papers,* William S. Myers, ed. (New York: Doubleday, 1934, 2 volumes), I, 189.

154 THE FATEFUL TURN

On the score of individualism, Hoover said that it had
been sturdy individuals who had made America great.
He declared that "the way to the Nation's greatness is
the path of self-reliance, independence, and steadfast-
ness in times of trial and stress."[9] The effort of American society should be to "safeguard to every individual
an equality of opportunity to take that position in the
community to which his intelligence, character, ability,
and ambition entitle him. . . ."[10] There must be no special privilege in America. Every individual must be free
to move from the lowest rung of society to the highest,
regardless of hereditary or financial background. The
function of government is "to assure to the individual
. . . liberty, justice, intellectual welfare, equality of opportunity, and stimulation to service."[11]

Hoover insisted, too, that individuals must be not only
free but responsible as well; indeed, such responsibility
is a condition of their freedom. The individual must first
of all have moral standards. He must have a sense of
duty, obligation, and responsibility. It is the duty of
the citizen to give service to his country, to exercise his
franchise and thus participate in government, to care
for those unable to care for themselves. Hoover insisted,
however, that these responsibilities for aiding the needy
should fall directly upon the individual, that something
was forever gone from charity if it were made a function of government. It would become divorced from giving out of the warmth of the heart and become inextri-

---

[9] *Ibid.,* p. 568.

[10] Herbert Hoover, *American Individualism* (New York:
Doubleday, 1922), pp. 9-10.

[11] *Ibid.,* p. 19.

cably bound up with the cold business of taxation and legislation.

Hoover: the Progressive

Thus far, it would appear that Hoover was a thoroughgoing individualist. There is, however, another side to both his writings and his public actions. He was also to some indefinable extent a Progressive. In effect, this meant that he accepted the analysis that conditions had changed in America, and that these changes called for a great deal more cooperative action than had been the case in earlier America. It meant that Hoover attempted to make a great compromise between individualism and collectivism. He tried to steer a course between voluntarism and coercive government action in the solution of problems. But such middle ground does not exist.

Nor should it be thought that Hoover's progressivism resulted from a battlefield conversion during the depression. On the contrary, as Secretary of Commerce he advocated measures which indicate his "liberal" attitude toward the role of the government in the economy. One of the problems which arose—or was raised—as early as 1922 was whether or not to regulate an entirely new medium, radio. Hoover came out in that year for federal regulation of the ether,[12] arguing that both monopolistic control and anarchistic exploitations must be prevented. The principle underlying this control was to be that the "ether is a public medium, and its use must be for the public benefit. The use of a radio channel is jus-

---

[12] See Herbert Hoover, "Policing the Ether," *Scientific American,* CXXVII (August, 1922), 80.

tified only if there is public benefit. The dominant element for consideration in the radio field is, and always will be, the great body of the listening public."[13]

During the same period, he declared that one of the major problems of agriculture was the lack of cheap transportation. To remedy this situation, he proposed that a national program involving both the federal and state governments be launched to develop inland waterways and rivers.[14] In the field of regulation, Hoover requested that the federal government regulate the activities of fishermen off the shores of the United States and Alaska so that a perpetual supply of fish would be available. He wanted the government also to replenish or restore the supply of certain fish which were disappearing because of overfishing.[15]

In the matter of trade, Hoover was a protectionist. In his campaign for the Presidency, he said: "I advocate strengthening of the protective tariff as Henry Clay of Kentucky; not as an abstract economic theory, but as a practical and definite policy of protecting the standards of living of the American family."[16] He favored a selective use of the tariff to bolster and maintain the American economy. The test for tariff revision is "whether there has been a substantial slackening of activity in an industry during the past few years, and a consequent

[13] Herbert Hoover, *Memoirs* (New York: Macmillan, 1951-52, 3 volumes), II, 144.

[14] Herbert Hoover, "Waterways—the Farmer's Need," *The Country Gentleman*, XCI (number 3), 3-4.

[15] Hoover, *Memoirs*, II, 150-153.

[16] Herbert Hoover, *The New Day* (Stanford: Stanford University Press, 1928), pp. 101-02.

decrease of employment due to insurmountable competition in the products of that industry."[17]

On the matter of taxation, Hoover tacked to and fro
over the years. He affirmed his belief, on one occasion,
that the federal tax system "should be revised to accomplish definite social and economic objectives. . . ."[18] One
of these objectives, it would appear from what he said
elsewhere, would be a redistribution of the wealth.
"Luck and genius create large fortunes. But the inherit-
ance of great economic power by descendants is not consonant with a free people."[19] He stated his belief in the
payment according to means, "My administration having more than doubled the upper brackets of the income
taxes up to 55 per cent. . . ."[20] Actually, however, the
record for the time shows that Hoover opposed corporate
taxes and the raising of the income tax rates.[21] In fact,
Hoover did not stand on principle but rather tried to
keep income and corporate taxes low on the expedient
grounds that such taxes dried up the sources of capital.

The major proof for Hoover's compromise, however,
lies in the measures which he favored to combat the depression. He did say on several occasions that the government could not legislate the United States out of a
depression.[22] On the other hand, he held that the federal
government should take positive action to strengthen the
economic institutions of the country, to insure that the

---

[17] Hoover, *State Papers,* I, 35.

[18] Hoover, *Addresses,* IV, 229.

[19] *Ibid.,* I, 198.

[20] *Ibid.,* p. 193.

[21] See Hoover, *State Papers,* II, 200, 580; *Memoirs,* III,
137.

[22] See Hoover, *State Papers,* I, 429-30, 515, 578.

deserving needy should not suffer, to make every effort
to hold wages and living standards up, and to aid agriculture in a critical period.

To provide relief for farmers, Hoover proposed a number of measures, most of which were implemented by
Congress. The Hawley-Smoot tariff was supposed to secure the domestic market to American farmers by raising rates covering agricultural products. To provide
cheaper transportation, a treaty was made with Canada
that opened the way for the development of the St. Law-
rence waterway. Hoover proposed that the Federal Land
Banks be reorganized to facilitate the refinancing of
farm mortgages.

The most sweeping innovation was the Federal Farm
Board, which was created to coordinate and give material assistance to farmers. During his campaign in 1928
Hoover declared that the proposed board "should have
power to determine the facts, the causes, the remedies
which should be applied to each and every one of the
multitude of problems which we mass under the general
term 'the agricultural problem.' "[23] The major part of
this program, that part embodied in the Agricultural
Marketing Act, was designed to facilitate cooperative
marketing. To this end, it was to develop clearing-houses
for farm products, provide warehouse facilities for
storage, and eliminate waste in distribution. "But in
particular the board is to build up, with initial advances
of capital from the government, farmer-owned and
farmer-controlled . . . corporations which will protect
the farmer from depression."[24] Direct relief and loans

---

[23] Hoover, *The New Day,* pp. 194-95.
[24] *Ibid.,* p. 115.

during the period of 1930 through 1932 rose from $156,100,000 in 1930 to $772,700,000 in 1932.

A far reaching program of public works was undertaken during Hoover's administration. While Hoover later heatedly denied that government could spend its way out of depression, he approved and advanced programs to do just that. Beginning in 1930 and going through 1933 over two and one-third billions of dollars were spent on public works. There was an increase in amounts from $410,420,000 in 1930 to $717,260,000 in 1933.

Hoover tried to use the office of the President to get businessmen to hold the wage level at its then current level. Indeed, as Secretary of Commerce he had attempted to get businessmen to reduce hours of work in order to increase employment. He called a meeting with business leaders in 1929, and they agreed to maintain the status quo in wages and employment.

He also approved definite substantial government aid to businesses to bolster the economy. Home loan banks were set up to aid credit institutions and encourage new home construction and individual home ownership. A National Credit Corporation, to rediscount notes that the Federal Reserve banks would not handle, was organized by credit institutions. The most far-reaching of the government programs was the Reconstruction Finance Corporation. Its purpose was to make "loans for income producing and self-sustaining enterprises which will increase employment whether undertaken by public bodies or by private enterprises."[25] On March 25, 1932, a few

---

[25] Hoover, *State Papers*, II, 187-88.

weeks after it had been chartered, the RFC had made loans to 587 banks and trust companies, 18 building and loan associations, 13 insurance companies, 13 railroads, 2 joint stock land banks, 3 mortgage loan companies, 1 livestock credit association, and a large loan to the Secretary of Agriculture.

The character of the compromise begins to emerge. Hoover disapproved many of the programs that were being proposed for government aid. In general, the programs he did approve were voluntary, so far as active participation in them was concerned. The money involved was much more apt to be extended as a loan than as a grant. Of course, the taxpayer who provided these funds did not do so voluntarily, at least not as an individual. But Hoover was attempting to use positive government action within the framework of the American tradition, as he understood it.

Principles Abandoned

Hoover's compromise failed. All agree upon that, though there are differences of opinion as to why it failed. Those who believe in full-fledged government action maintain that he did not go far enough. Those who question the melioristic efforts themselves will see that Hoover's half-way house was neither fish nor fowl, and think that he may have delayed recovery by interfering in the economy and holding out a false hope.

By compromising, Hoover had departed from the basic principles of individualism. He had, implicitly at least, proclaimed that government was responsible for economic conditions. By acting along these lines, he established precedents for and expectations of such action. He could, and did, protest loudly against the more thoroughgoing and coercive actions of the Roosevelt administration, but the ground under his feet was shaky. Once enter upon government spending to stimulate the economy, and where do you draw the line against such spending? Once admit that government must act positively to rescue people from the effects of depression, and what are the limits of that responsibility? They are only such as opinion may decree. The experience of the twentieth century would indicate that once governments are launched on their melioristic courses they rarely turn back short of socialism. Demands mount for more and more such action, and the thing picks up bulk and momentum like a snowball going down hill. There is no return short of a return to principle.

Politics is indeed the art of compromise. But two things need to be kept in mind in this regard. First, in whose direction is the compromise being made? It should be clear that the man who opposes reforms gains only a temporary stay of execution when he compromises in the matter of the degree of the reform. A libertarian could favor a compromise that would make participation in Social Security voluntary, for he favors voluntary action and he would be moving in the direction of the eventual abolition of Social Security. But to effect a compromise which extends compulsory Social Security only to housewives rather than to housewives and handymen is but to yield ground, with the near certainty that the next time around the handymen will receive coverage.

The other point is that the principle of limited government does not envisage political action in all things. It rather sees government restricted to a very narrow sphere of action. It follows, then, that when we say that politics is the art of compromise, we do not mean that everything is subject to such compromises. Compromise is only appropriate regarding the legitimate concerns of government.

10.

The Half-Way House

COMPROMISE FAILED in the 1930's to preserve the individualistic way. This is not surprising, for the beliefs which undergirded individualism had already been largely eroded away. Those who defended the older way were scorned as "neanderthals," "reactionaries," and "moss-backs," rather pathetic creatures who had not kept up with the "times." There was a measure of truth to this charge, for they had ceased to describe new ways by which individuals might grapple with and solve their problems. Few there were who could turn the charges of the "liberals" and present coherently a counter version of reality. The truth was that many would-be defenders, like Hoover, had drunk deeply at the fountain of Progressivism and the charge of backwardness was hard to bear. Thus, they yielded ground to take on some of the protective coloration of liberalism. Hoover's *Memoirs* are an excellent example of such an apology.

But compromises plus the holding actions of conservatives did result in something else—what I am calling here a half-way house. By the mid-1950's this new position, if position it is, had taken shape. It has been called by many names: the welfare state, social democracy, democratic liberalism, and humane capitalism. It

is, according to its adherents, somewhere between individualism and collectivism, between capitalism and
communism, between individual liberty and social security. It is the house of the mixed economy, of positive
government, of world-wide social concern, of affluence
and generosity.

The champions of this half-way house range across
the spectrum of American political positions, are to be
found among labor union leaders and businessmen, and
have in recent years crowded aggressively toward the
center, proclaiming theirs the middle-of-the-road. A typical example of this kind of thinking can be found in a
little book written by Arthur M. Schlesinger, Jr., called,
befuddlingly enough since he is admittedly of the left,
The Vital Center. This center of which he speaks is the
mixed society which has emerged in the twentieth century to confound both communists and capitalists.

In Schlesinger's words, "The liberal democratic state
. . . has brought about a redistribution of wealth which
has defeated Marx's prediction of ever-worsening economic crisis. What the democratic parties of the developed nations have done, in short, has been to use the
state to force capitalism to do what both the classical
capitalists and the classical Marxists declared was impossible. . . ." According to him it was an uphill battle
all the way. "Nonetheless they persevered; and the
twentieth century in America and Great Britain saw the
rejection of laissez-faire, the subjugation of the business
cycle, the drowning of revolution in a torrent of consumer goods. . . ." The good society came about in the
following manner, according to this interpreter. "The
revolutionary fires within capitalism, lit by the great

industrialists in the nineteenth century, were put out in the twentieth by the triumphs of industry—and by the liberal politicians, by Theodore Roosevelt and Woodrow Wilson and Franklin D. Roosevelt. Such men ignored the dogmatists, the philosophers of either/or, and created the mixed society."[1]

The triumph of this new way, according to Schlesinger, came in a burst of glory with the inauguration of Franklin D. Roosevelt. "Since that March day in 1933, one has been able to feel that liberal ideas had access to power in the United States, that liberal purposes, in general, were dominating our national policy. . . . It has stood for responsibility and for achievement, not for frustration and sentimentalism; it has been the instrument of social change, not of private neurosis."[2]

There are a great many people, no doubt, who would question that Schlesinger stands at the center of anything except his own ego. And certainly there have been numerous other claimants to the middle-of-the-road position who do not share his perspective. Clinton Rossiter has recently stated an almost unchallengable position of the center. He says, "My own position . . . is that of a man who is in principle well removed from Dr. Peale in the direction of Dr. Niebuhr and well removed from Russell Kirk in the direction of Walter Lippmann, in politics well to the right of Walter Reuther and well to the left of Senator Goldwater." Indeed, he is so comfortably situated in the half-way house that he "wishes

---

[1] Arthur M. Schlesinger, Jr., *The Vital Center* (Boston: Houghton Mifflin, Sentry Edition, 1962), p. xii.

[2] *Ibid.*, pp. xxi-xxii.

the conservatives almost as well as he wishes the liberals. . . ."[3]

National Goals

Perhaps the best of all statements by occupants of the half-way house is that of the Report of the President's Commission on National Goals. This Commission was appointed by President Eisenhower, and its Report is available to us in both clothbound and paperback editions as *Goals for Americans*.[4] The Commission, chaired by Dr. Henry M. Wriston, had eleven members ranging from former college presidents to a labor leader. They hopefully adumbrate a future, viewed from the half-way house, in which no hard choices have to be made. We shall be able to have all that we want without giving up anything significant. We can have social security without losing individual liberty, government aid without government control, receive help from groups to provide the intimate necessities of life and retain our independence.

The book contains many professions of devotion to the individual, his freedom, fulfillment, and protection. Regarding the primary importance of the individual, it says:

> The status of the individual must remain our primary concern. All our institutions—political, social, and economic—must further enhance the dignity of

[3] Clinton Rossiter, *Conservatism in America* (New York: Alfred A. Knopf, Second Edition Revised, 1962), pp. viii-ix.

[4] My references will be to the paperback edition published by Prentice Hall as A Spectrum Book.

the citizen, promote the maximum development of his capabilities, stimulate their responsible exercise, and widen the range and effectiveness of opportunities for individual choice. (p. 3.)

Respect for the individual means respect for every individual. (p. 4.)

The degree of effective liberty available to its people should be the ultimate test for any nation. (p. 4.)

Individuals should have maximum freedom in their choice of jobs, goods, and services. (p. 9.)

The above were taken from that part of the Report which was a joint effort. There are chapters in the book by individuals, and they too contain many references of concern for the individual and for liberty.

Dr. Henry M. Wriston, in the chapter on "The Individual," says:

One man's freedom should involve no trespass upon others' rights to life, liberty, and the pursuit of happiness. (p. 50.)
The acid test of successful democratic government is the degree of effective liberty it makes available to the individual." (p. 48.)

Clinton Rossiter, in the selection called "The Democratic Process," declares:

The price of liberty, today as through all history, is self-reliance and self-discipline. (p. 76.)

Dr. John W. Gardner, "National Goals in Education," maintains:

Our deepest convictions impel us to foster individual fulfillment. We wish each one to achieve the promise that is in him. (p. 81.)

If we knew no more than this about the book on *Goals for Americans,* we might conclude that it is a new declaration of independence cast in the mold of romantic individualism. There is little, if any, in what I have quoted to which Benjamin Franklin, Thomas Jefferson, George Mason, Richard Henry Lee, or Ralph Waldo Emerson might have objected. One might expect that the concrete proposals of the Commission would be along the lines of the reduction of governmental operations, limitations of the powers of regulatory commissions, curtailment of the taxing powers of government, restoration of the responsibility of parents for their children, and an increase of privately initiated, financed, and managed activities. But such ideas are given short shrift in the half-way house.

Intervention Recommended

By what means does the Report seek to implement its professed concern for individual liberty, free enterprise, the fulfillment of the individual, and the like? The Commission recommends increased government spending, government manipulation of thought, maintenance of regulation, and, in general, extensions of the collective effort. Some excerpts will indicate this:

> One role of government is to stimulate changes of attitude. (p. 4.)
> Greater resources—private, corporate, municipal, state, and federal—must be mobilized. A higher proportion of the gross national product must be devoted to educational purposes. (p. 6.)
> The economy should grow at the maximum rate consistent with primary dependence upon free enter-

prise and the avoidance of marked inflation. Increased investment in the public sector is compatible with this goal. (p. 10.)

Government programs of help for farmers, including price supports and other means to prevent collapse of incomes, will continue to be necessary for some time; they must be so managed that they cushion the shock of the transition, without unduly slowing the pace of necessary fundamental adjustments. (p. 13.)

We must remedy slum conditions, reverse the process of decay in the large cities, and relieve the necessity for low-income and minority groups to concentrate there.

We should also seek solutions for haphazard suburban growth, and provide an equitable sharing of the cost of public services between central cities and suburbs. (p. 13.)

Federal grants for the construction of hospitals should be continued and extended to other medical facilities. Increased private, state, and federal support is necessary for training doctors. (p. 14.)

In addition, there should be established a federal reinsurance program for states with temporary acute employment problems. Public and private arrangements for maintaining income during sickness should be improved. (p. 15.)

The character of the Report begins to manifest itself. It pays lip service to such traditional American ideals as freedom for the individual, individual fulfillment, free enterprise, and individual responsibility. It makes concrete proposals, however, for collective responsibility, government stimulation and planning for the economy, urban renewal with the aid of the national purse, and national more often than individual fulfillment.

It tells us something about the half-way house, too. It suggests that it is a stopping point, not the final destination. But let us return to this later after we have examined some related developments.

However much repair and improvement may be called for by the tenants of the half-way house, it has nonetheless become the fortress of the faith, and its tenets have become the basis for an orthodoxy. It is the citadel of defense against communism on the left and capitalism on the right. Most of its inhabitants have turned from agitation for radical reform to the more domestic task of keeping the faith.

The Reform Effort

When did this transformation of the reform impetus take place? To answer this question we need to review the course of the development of the melioristic reform movement and its establishment in American life. The clamor for this kind of reform became audible for the first time in the latter part of the nineteenth century. There was a mounting tide of criticism of the "plutocracy," of vested interests, of the inequality of the distribution of the wealth, of business immorality, and so forth. Native reformers were joined by foreign devotees of various ideologies: socialism, communism, anarchism. Reformers found the most fertile soil for the cultivation of their reforms among the economically discontented, among farmers and industrial laborers mainly. Various attempts were made to forge these disparate efforts into a political party, but these failed, to be buried in history as third parties.

The reform effort began to meet with success when it was absorbed by or merged with the major parties. The Democratic party adopted a great deal of the Populist program and became spokesman for much of the rural discontent in 1896 and afterward. Reformers became an important element of the Republican party in the early years of the twentieth century as Progressives or Insurgents. Presidents—particularly Theodore Roosevelt and Woodrow Wilson—began to speak the language of reform. But reformers were only able to forward a few innovations in the early twentieth century, and following World War I the reform effort was stymied.

The triumph of reform came, of course, with the election and programs of Franklin D. Roosevelt. During the 1930's, however, the reform ideas had not yet become an orthodoxy. They were advanced as emergency measures in the shadow of depression. Proclaimed necessity rather than desirability was the professed occasion for their adoption. Their establishment as an orthodoxy came more gradually. Roosevelt's election to third and fourth terms gave unprecedented popular sanction to him and by extension to his programs. Truman's upset victory over Dewey in 1948 provided a further aura of permanence to the reform measures of the Democratic party.

It was the apparent acceptance of these reforms by Republicans during the Eisenhower years that presaged their becoming an orthodoxy. President Eisenhower did not press for the repeal of the reforms of the Roosevelt and Truman administrations. He did harbor for awhile the mutters of discontent with some of them, but in the main he not only accepted them but began tentatively

172 THE FATEFUL TURN

to extend the earlier reforms, to the accompanying applause of "liberals." When this happened, the orthodoxy was established.

Adjusting to the New Order

That such an orthodoxy exists has been difficult to detect. Those who advanced the reforms initially have thought of and proclaimed themselves perpetual reformers. The very concept of orthodoxy is repugnant to them. Did they not unseat the older way by relativistic, experimental, and pragmatic methods and arguments? Have they not ever avowed the necessity for continuous change and adjustment before the flux of circumstances? Were they not the ones who argued for the flexibility of the Constitution, for the relativity of morals, for the necessity of fronting new experiences with an open mind, for the tendency of groups in power to rationalize their private aggrandizement as public benefaction? The answer to these questions is yes, but it serves now to shield the "liberal" from his own orthodoxy.

Perhaps the best sign of the existence of an orthodoxy is the attitude toward dissenters from it. Few, if any, established faiths really have any place for those who disagree verbally with them. Certainly, "liberalism" does not have. Dissent must be inactivated or it must be crushed. The inhabitants of the half-way house do not usually approve of crushing opponents by force, though the Meredith Affair in Mississippi suggests they are losing their qualms on this score. But they have been too long the proponents of freedom of speech to abandon the position quickly. Besides, it is an article of faith among the orthodox that their way does not involve the loss of any significant "freedoms." At any rate, thus far they have attempted to dispose of dissenters by inactivating them.

More specifically, a vocabulary has been developed for denouncing the more bellicose of the dissenters and for making them pariahs among decent men. They are called extremists, irresponsibles, ultranationalists, members of the radical right, immoderates, and the like. Obviously, one does not carry on discourse with such people, and they are in this manner put beyond the pale. But more important, this language is eloquent of the existence of an orthodoxy. "Responsible," in this context, means one who is working, acting, and speaking to effectuate the aims of the prevailing order.

The less belligerent dissenters are dealt with more gently. One of the favorite devices for disposing of them is by psychologizing about their condition. Here is a mild example given by an historian trying to account for the supporters of Senator Taft in the post-World War II period:

> These malcontents were as much a product of the Half-Century of Revolution as the situations which annoyed them so much. All during the years since the 1890's, the emerging society had been making enemies. Many of those foes were members of the high-income strata, who saw the period as one long aggravating process of redistributing their wealth. . . .
> Yet the grievance was not wholly economic. . . . The Half-Century of Revolution, particularly the jolting changes since 1933, had been a trial to all those whose temperaments yearned for stability. . . . Now

the established classes were having to make room for groups from the bottom and they were feeling uncomfortable, jostled, almost displaced in an America which they had assumed belonged to them.[5]

Poor things, one gathers, they are more to be pitied than censured for their difficulties in adjusting to this Brave New World! This is perhaps an even more effective device for disposing of dissenters than invective.

Rewriting History

The prevalence of an orthodoxy is evinced, too, in the current rewriting of history. In the early twentieth century, it will be recalled, historians and others defamed the American tradition. The Constitution was described as a "bundle of compromises," and the authors of it as busily forwarding their class interests. The American heroes were debunked, the American way villified, and the American businessman denigrated. Individualism was rationalized selfishness and the resort to free enterprise arguments the first resort of scoundrels.

Such arguments served very well to destroy the older American way, but when "liberalism" had been established, something else was needed. Since about 1940, then, the writing of history has taken a different course. Historians have busied themselves in rewriting American history to show that the half-way house has been the vision pulling Americans onward from the outset, that it is the culmination of the American dream (or

---

[5] Eric F. Goldman, *The Crucial Decade and After* (New York: Vintage, 1960), p. 53.

will be, when the House is finished), and that it is in keeping with the "real" American tradition. So thoroughly have they done their work that it is by now a cliché that Americans have always been distinguished by pragmatic and experimental practices.

While they have been busy squeezing the new orthodoxy into the American tradition, however, most historians have left off reinterpreting recent American history. Accounts of the New Deal tend to read like press releases from the White House (when Roosevelt was in it). The story of the coming of and American participation in World War II is little altered from the front page versions of the time. The language of necessity with which politicians justify their behavior fast becomes the language by which historians write apologies for events. Nor should it go unremarked that these things are a betrayal of the task of the historian. The greatest of the public functions of the historian is to notify us out of his sensitivity to the past when we are breaking with it. But when he is busily showing us that each new step is in keeping with the tradition, he has ceased to perform his proper function.

So well established as an orthodoxy are the creed and practices of the half-way house that older labels are now being applied to the inhabitants. Thus, one may now be classed as a liberal or conservative regarding the programs of "liberalism." Clinton Rossiter, as I suggested earlier, has been carving out a niche for conservatives among "liberals." Those like Russell Kirk and William F. Buckley who call themselves conservatives are in reality pseudoconservatives according to his view. In the quest for the true conservative, he tells us, the "ultraconservatives, despite their deeply conservative urges, must be counted out of this particular search, for most of them have fallen prey to two failings against which conservatives must be constantly on guard: first, an inability to accept gracefully social and economic changes that have been firmly established in a successful way of life . . . ; second, a weakness for arguments and methods that unravel the bonds of social unity."[6]

The true conservatives, according to Rossiter, are those who follow such policies as those of Eisenhower and Taft, "for they are aimed squarely at preserving a successful way of life; conservative in method, for they steer a prudent course between too much progress, which throws us into turmoil, and too little. . . ."[7] In short, the half-way house is the only dwelling available, or so he would have us think, and the only viable question is whether one shall take up residence in the left wing or the right wing.

The New Ideology

In discussing the impact of the Great Depression upon Americans, Alfred Kazin says: "For whether interpreted as a breakdown of capitalism or a visitation from on high, a temporary failure of institutions or the epilogue to America's participation in the First World War, the crisis imposed with catastrophic violence what other national experiences had induced slowly and indirectly —a new conception of reality."[8]

---

[6] Rossiter, *op. cit.*, p. 177.

[7] *Ibid.*, p. 180.

[8] Kazin, *On Native Grounds*, p. 283.

Now it would be more accurate to say that the depression provided the opportunity for the triumph of a new conception of reality. But phraseology aside, let us all agree that 1933 marked a decisive turning point in American history. The jerry-built structure of the half-way house was erected hastily in the months and years following March of 1933. It was erected upon the sands that had been gathered for half a century, however. To put it more directly, the orthodoxy of the 1950's and 1960's rests upon an ideology which men began shaping in the latter part of the nineteenth century. I have described this ideology as it took shape in chapter 5, but here I would like to discuss it again as it has hardened into an orthodoxy.

An ideology is a complex of interrelated ideas containing an implicit and completed version of reality. It carries with it a blueprint of the good (or perfect) society and the means for its achievement. The ideas composing it may have been assembled from many sources, but once they have become an ideology no one of them may be subtracted or greatly altered without destroying or calling into question the whole.

The word "ideology" should not, however, be used casually to describe any set of beliefs. This is to adopt the current procedure of confounding all things. Like so much of current terminology, this is a word given currency by the Marxists. Most specifically, it is the view that ideas derive from sense perceptions of matter; it is a profoundly materialistic conception. It took on, too, the color of utopianism and the building of an earthly paradise. Those who innocently use "ideology" to refer to all philosophies, theologies, sets of principles, and

systems of belief are unwittingly innoculating their
hearers against a sensitivity to a particular kind of system of beliefs. When I say that the half-way house is
founded upon an ideology, then, I mean to convey the
idea that it rests upon a system of beliefs which are
utopian and materialistic in character.

The utopia which this ideology holds out as a vision
is altogether pleasant and enticing. It is of a place and
time where suffering and privation have been banished,
where the inhabitants are secure from the ravages of
disease and unemployment, where all men have enough
of the good things of life and none have too much,
where education and environment have banished the
baser things and men have willingly and gladly turned
to the finer things of life, where one may speed in a
carefree manner down the highway of life with no fear
of a collision along the way. It is true that this vision
of utopia has been dimmed by the course of twentieth
century developments and the guides have careworn
faces because of the responsibilities that have devolved
upon them in providing this utopia, but it still lurks in
the back of the mind of the most hard-bitten intellectual of the movement and usually erupts in bright col-
ors when the politician makes his promises for what
his administration will accomplish.

This utopia was to be realized by a gradual and un-
ending progress upward. Thus, the idea of progress is
one of the central component ideas of the ideology.
From this perspective, the inhabitants of the half-way
house can be called progressives. The progressive believes that the direction of civilization is mainly along
the lines that it should be and that American society is

essentially sound. He generally deplores unfavorable critiques of his civilization and is inclined to the view that their propagators are cranks. He supports the central developments of the twentieth century: industrialization, automation, mass production, mass media of communication, rapid transportation, the compiling of data by scientists, internationalism, and the breaking down of regionalism and localism. He approves the centralization of authority, rationalization of the economy, the homogenization of the population (removal of local, racial, religious, or any other group distinguishing features), and increases in public services provided by governmental agencies. All of these he is apt to associate with progress. Those twentieth century developments which he disapproves—totalitarianism, total war, mass destruction—he views as aberrations from, not as integral concomitants to, those developments which he approves.

Exponents of the progressive position have a virtual monopoly of the media of communication. They are publishers of many of the popular newspapers and magazines, occupy prominent chairs in centers of higher learning, make movies and television programs, occupy prestigious pulpits, originate much of the advertising, interpret the news, and in general set the tone and attempt to provide the approved attitudes for Americans. At the present time the progressives appear to dominate both of the major political parties in the United States, work out the legislative programs, and make the court decisions on a national level.

The progressive is confident of the beneficence of most twentieth century developments. He recognizes threats to his security in world communism, atomic warfare, totalitarianism, complacency, ignorance, inequalities of wealth, hunger, unemployment, and disease. If the progressive is an intellectual, he can get the solutions to the problems from Walter Lippmann, Arthur Schlesinger, Jr., John Kenneth Galbraith, and Bertrand Russell. If he is not, he can acquire more digestible doses from Drew Pearson, Walter Winchell, and Norman Vincent Peale. The middle-of-the-road progressive can get his weekly sustenance from *Time,* and if reading is too painful, there is always *Life* to present the message in pictures—the strained, hurt visage of Eisenhower beside the bellicose, vituperative Khrushchev.

Blueprint for Progress

But I digress. The common denominator of the progressives is their belief that the major problems confronting mankind can be solved by international cooperation, foreign aid, popular government, education, research, greater productivity, industrialization, governmental planning, and greater interest and participation in public affairs.

The progressive is not much concerned with forms and institutions, as such. The main danger, he thinks, is that we will not continue the progress of the last hundred years at an ever more rapid pace. The important thing to the progressive is the solution of our remaining problems by more progress in extending understanding among people, in removing space and time as obstacles to communication and travel, in removing ignorance by education, in providing plenty through productivity. The progressive is condescending toward the past, inclined to pity those who lived in less advanced times. He believes that times change and that we are better equipped to deal with changes as we are unhampered by customs, traditions, and forms—the dead weight of the past.

This is, of course, the idea of progress welded into the half-way house, made a part of the "liberal" ideology. One may, of course, admire and approve of certain developments of the modern era without taking this ideology. But once one accepts the central premise of automatic progress he is impelled toward accepting what now is as the best that ever was, and that includes the present order in the society.

Progressivism is, however, mainly the impulsive and justificatory side of the ideology. One of the main ingredients, as I indicated in an earlier chapter, is the organic conception of society. Applied, this has resulted in a new conception of reality. It has resulted in an attempt to create a social morality rather than an individual one. It is a social morality of social responsibilities and duties, of loyalty to a social unit, of significance in terms of one's contribution to society. It is very difficult to enunciate this new morality, and such enunciations as have been made of it have produced confusions.

The classic case of confusion arising from this new morality was President Kennedy's words to the effect that we should ask not what our country could do for us but what we could do for it. In characterizing his New Frontier, he elaborated this idea, declaring that it "is not a set of promises; it is a set of challenges. It sums up not what I intend to offer to the American people, but what I intend to ask of them. It holds out the promise of more sacrifices instead of more security."[9]

What were the sacrifices to be? Legislatively, he has called for federally supported health insurance for the aged, for federal aid to education, for aid to distressed areas, for federal investigation of the sources of juvenile delinquency, and so forth. Thus, he has been chided by editorial writers with departing from his precept. Yet it is likely that the writers are mistaken; they have not understood the new morality. Society as an organism sacrifices collectively, not as lone individuals. The sacrifices are in the realm of taxation, service in the armed forces, giving as a nation to other peoples. If this does not quite make sense, it is probably because some remnants of the old morality still prevail to distort the vision. At any rate, the organic conception of society provides the vantage point of the new ideology.

From National Socialism to Empires

The bounds of the social organism are capable of considerable compression or extension. In thought and plan they have ranged from Robert Dale Owen's visionary self-sufficient community at New Harmony to Wendell Willkie's *One World*. Groups or classes have also been conceived as social organisms, and this conception was rather strong earlier in labor movements. However, only three conceptions of the social organism prevail today: the nation, the Free World, and the United Nations.

---

[9] *Time*, LXXVI (July 25, 1960), 10.

Socialism (or the welfare state) has come almost everywhere in the twentieth century via the route of nationalism. This is true of the Soviet Union as it is of the United States. There is considerable irony in this, for socialists have generally been the most vigorous antinationalists—the first to confidently predict that the day of the nation-state is over. But there is an explanation for this. Much of the world was organized in nation-states as socialism came to the fore; hence, socialists used the prevailing organizations. In order to begin to take collectivist action, however, it was useful to be insulated from the world market, the international effect of the gold standard, the products and trade of other countries. In short, the old internationalism had to be negated before socialism could be effected. This was done by slamming down iron curtains: raising tariff barriers, controlling immigration, going off the gold standard, and making trade agreements from country to country. This allowed countries to begin to manage currencies effectively.

Thus, the welfare state came as a kind of national socialism, and this is still its most prominent feature, at least in the United States. This nation-as-social-organism is evidenced in the language of national income, national wealth, national health, national defense, and of the competition among nations in various realms. However, collectivists, as a matter of doctrine, believe in the extension of the boundaries of the social organism, bit by bit if necessary, until it embraces the whole world. Currently, the Soviet Union is the center of one such extension, and the United States the center of another. The United Nations represents what, in the cur-

rent climate of opinion, would be the instrument of an
international (or world) social organism. The current
tendency, however, is much more of a thrust toward the
formation of empires in an almost traditional sense
than it is toward the formation of one world. Foreign
aid—government to government loans—in the half-way
house may be both an instrument of international socialism and a device for extending the influence of and
defending the United States.

Democratic Methods

The method of this collectivist ideology is democratic.
Populism went into the formation of the ideology, and
the belief that democratic procedures legitimate any
action is an absolute. Democracy was the key word in
the promulgation of the welfare state, particularly during the heady days of the 1930's. The argument ran
something like this: The United States is a democracy.
In a democracy the people are sovereign and whatever
is done for the good of the people is justified. Limited
government, as embodied in the Constitution, had been
a device for thwarting the will of the people and preventing action for the general welfare. Under the impetus of these ideas, the Constitution was reconstrued
and the limits which it imposed largely overridden. Democracy, as used by New Dealers, was informed by the
organic conception of society, and the "people" conceived not as individuals but as classes and masses.
The operative phrase was the greatest good for the
greatest number, and in terms of the ideology and of
social and economic circumstances this meant, largely,

an advancement of the masses at the expense of the classes. These are, of course, gross terms for characterizing programs of social security, government loans for farm and home buying, devaluation of the currency, the progressive income tax, privileges extended to organized labor and farmers. Thus, the method by which the welfare state was erected was called democratic.

Rights were given an entirely new meaning in this ideology. They were creations of the imagination and granted by the state. These new rights were ably summed up and set forth by President Franklin D. Roosevelt in his Annual Message to Congress in 1944. He said, in part:

In our day these economic truths have become accepted as self-evident. We have accepted, so to speak, a second Bill of Rights under which a new basis of security and prosperity can be established for all—regardless of station, race or creed.

Among these are:

The right to a useful and remunerative job in the industries or shops or farms or mines of the nation;

The right to earn enough to provide adequate food and clothing and recreation;

The right of every farmer to raise and sell his products at a return which will give him and his family a decent living;

The right of every business man, large and small, to trade in an atmosphere of freedom from unfair competition and domination by monopolies at home or abroad;

The right of every family to a decent home;

The right to adequate medical care and the opportunity to achieve and enjoy good health;

The right to adequate protection from the eco-

nomic fears of old age, sickness, accident and unemployment;
The right to a good education.[10]

These "rights" are to be provided or guaranteed by
governments acting *positively* to insure them. Another
aspect of the ideology is the belief in an activist and
popular government. Such rights as these would, of
course, require extensive government planning and manipulation of the economy. The half-way house is the
partially planned society, done under the auspices of
the central government.

Some Problems and Contradictions

Years in power and the movement of intellectual developments have led to the adding of other ingredients
to the ideology. There is less emphasis now, among
"advanced thinkers," upon the perfectibility of man or
upon an early achievement of utopia. Particularly in
foreign affairs, there is much talk of a struggle extending into the future with no immediately predictable
happy ending. It is typical of "liberal" historians that
they now ascribe the bright hopes fostered by New Freedom intellectuals to shortsighted *American* habits. One
historian says, "We are a people whose history has
made us the land of the swift, total solution, brought
about by ourselves alone. We faced a wilderness; we
hacked it down. We were vexed by slavery; we cut it
out of our system. . . . Americans were the more inclined

---

[10] Franklin D. Roosevelt, *Nothing to Fear*, Ben D. Zevin,
ed. (New York: Popular Library, 1961), p. 406.

to believe in the quick, total solution of any world problem because they were sure that the world was no great problem anyhow."[11]

How ingenious, to ascribe the simplicities of Wilsonian liberals to the American frontier experience! One may expect some day to find the failure of slum clearance to cure juvenile delinquency ascribed to some baleful weakness in the American tradition. But my point is that experience in power has brought a changed emphasis among the proponents of the ideology. There may, I gather, be at least a few "problems" with us for some time yet.

Is the half-way house what it purports to be? Is it a substantial structure or a mirage? Have these United States discovered a happy middle ground between individual liberty and social security? Is the welfare state a felicitous adaptation of the American tradition to the exigencies of the twentieth century? Has the formula been found for leaving sufficient control over property and wealth in the hands of individuals and yet so regulating and controlling its use as to insure an equal distribution of the wealth? Has socialism been abandoned by enlightened thinkers in favor of the mixed economy and the near egalitarian society? Have we found a way to have the best of collectivism and the choicest remains of individualism?

The proponents of the half-way house would have us think so. Yet the proposals they make and the actions they take tell a different story. Schlesinger informs us, at one point, that the "new radicalism," which he ob-

---

[11] Goldman, *The Crucial Decade,* pp. 113-14.

viously approves, "has returned in great part to the historic philosophy of liberalism—to a belief in the integrity of the individual, in the limited state, in due process of law, in empiricism and gradualism."[12] Yet he had just finished saying that "Britain has already submitted itself to social democracy; the United States will very likely advance in that direction through a series of New Deals, and the advance will be accelerated if the country fails to keep out of a depression."[13] He poses interesting alternatives: either we shall move toward socialism gradually through steps he recommends, or we shall move more quickly as a result of crises stemming from the ignoring of his advice. Despite the subtlety of the description, socialism is the wave of the future. It smells sweeter, Shakespeare to the contrary not withstanding, by being called a different name. If his version is accepted, we are not in a half-way house at all but on a slow train to socialism.

Commissions and Confusion

Or, let us return to the Report of the President's Commission on National Goals. The Report attempts to reconcile all contradictions and bring all viewpoints into the half-way house. It favors more governmental programs, but naturally it is opposed to greater centralization. For example:

> The federal government supports more than half of the research and development in the United States.

---

[12] Schlesinger, *The Vital Center,* p. 156.
[13] *Ibid.,* p. 154.

It is of urgent importance that the administration of its scientific and technical programs be strengthened, but without resort to bureaucratic overcentralization and planning. (p. 8.)

Is this to be an unplanned strengthening of the administration of the programs? When does bureaucratic centralization become "bureaucratic overcentralization"? It appears to me that the Commission is saying something like this: "Tighten the nut on the bolt, but leave it as loose as it now is." The Commission must have had in mind the example of the Defense Department, unified but separate, co-ordinated but each service acting in its own way!

Or consider this example of proposals to go in both directions at once. At one point, the Report of the Commission advocates the enlargement of "local discretion, as for example in the handling of matching federal grants. . . ." (p. 6.) Elsewhere they say, "The federal government should enforce the principle that federal funds shall not be disbursed to employers who discriminate on the basis of race. Similar policies should progressively be applied to federal grants for universities, hospitals, and airports, and to federal housing programs." (p. 4.) To state it abstractly, the Commission favors enlarging local discretion by increasing federal intervention. It is no wonder that men who reason thusly can believe that individual liberty can be promoted by governmental intervention, or that collective responsibility can be assumed for the well-being of each of us without any loss of individual initiative.

The confusion of these men is more apparent than real, however. Without questioning motives, I would

suggest that these men are not informed by the ideas
of individualism, even in modified form, whatever the
appearance to the contrary. Their tribute to the individual is only a pious pilgrimage to the grave of an an-
cestor. Their very willingness to draw up such comprehensive goals for the nation attests to the enfeeblement
of their individualism. Their concrete proposals involve
the increased activity of some collective, corporate, community, city, state, and/or national organization. Judging by what they recommend, no single activity can be
left solely to the individual; not unemployment insurance, nor the arts, nor the development of resources,
nor housing. There are no concrete proposals for protecting the individual from governments, despite the
vast increases in governmental activity which the Commission advocates. To the contrary, there are subtle
suggestions for removing such limitations as now exist
in the congressional power of appropriations, and in the
virtually unlimited debate in the Senate.

Social Necessities Come First

The very manner in which Dr. Henry M. Wriston, in
his chapter on "The Individual," defines the conflict between individual and social realms shows that his individualism is only vestigial. He says, "In a society so
completely, and complexly, organized as ours, in a
world so interdependent and so disturbed, the choice
between *individual desires* and *social necessities* becomes difficult." (p. 49, italics mine.) Who *would* care
to defend individual desires when social necessities are
in conflict with them? I had not supposed that an indi-

vidual's desires mattered to anyone except himself. Those who established the Republic thought in terms of the natural *rights* of the individual, not his *desires*.

It is plain in another instance that Dr. Wriston does not think in terms of individual rights. He declares, "Property and business exist for the benefit of individuals and have no inherent rights." (p. 52.) This is a truism and a circumlocution of the question it purports to raise. The question is not, nor should it ever have been, whether property has rights but whether *individuals* have rights to the use of the proceeds from the property which they own or rent. This is the central question about property with which individualism is concerned.

The Commission concludes its report by urging individuals to assume their responsibilities. One might suppose that the Commission would avow the primary responsibility of the individual for his own well-being. It should follow, then, that they would recommend such things as private savings against misfortune, the avoidance of indebtedness which limits independence, the securing of private property by which the individual might provide for his needs, and the restoration of primary responsibilities to the home.

They suggest no such things, of course. There is an oblique reference to the American's responsibility "for his own life and livelihood," but the concrete proposals which follow deal with our responsibilities to others. An individual who did devote himself primarily to his personal responsibilities would probably be condemned by the Commission's edict against "the fallacy of a purely selfish attitude—the materialistic ethic. Indifference to poverty and disease is inexcusable in a society dedicated to the dignity of the individual; so also is indifference to values other than material comfort and national power." (p. 23.) We are, instead, to assume responsibility for everyone else. "A basic goal for each American is to achieve a sense of responsibility as broad as his world-wide concerns and as compelling as the dangers and opportunities he confronts." (p. 23.) Apparently it does not trouble the Commission that individuals who cannot provide for their own private medical needs should assume the responsibilities of the whole world.

Man as a Natural Resource

Language, when not used in full consciousness of its import, can betray the true orientation of the writer. So it is with Dr. Wriston when he says, "The basic natural resource of the United States is its people. It follows inescapably that the first national goal to be pursued— at all levels, federal, state, local, and private—should be the development of each individual to his fullest potential." (p. 53.)

There are some "nice" words in the quotation which give the whole a soothing quality, but what is he saying? He is saying that the individual is a "natural resource," a resource of the nation, a subject for "national goals," something that is to be fully developed so that he can benefit us all. Fair words obscure the radical character of such thought. Does the individual exist for the nation, or does the nation exist for individuals? If I am a "natural resource of the United States," I must conclude that I exist for the state.

How far are these United States from their foundations when national leaders refer to human beings as
natural resources, when individual fulfillment has as
its end the meeting of national needs, when individual
responsibility is defined as responsibility for all mankind, when private property is subtly attacked in the
name of the individual, when the extension of collective activity is urged in the name of individual liberty?
Toward what kind of society would the "goals" of the
Commission take us (whether wittingly or not)? What
rights would remain for the individual in such a society?
Would it not be a society in which everyone is "developed" to his fullest (whether he will or no), in which
each is responsible for all and all are responsible for
each, in which it is one's "duty" to contribute signifi-
cantly to the general welfare? How much longer can
such a society permit the wasteful "laissez-faire" practice of individual choice of vocation? Lest I be accused
of imagining such dangers, note this pronouncement by
the Commission:

> We must use available manpower more efficiently.
> The practice of wasting highly trained people in jobs
> below their capacity . . . must be eliminated. (p. 8.)

Suppose I were to insist upon wasting my talents, would
I have to be eliminated also?

I deal here with the tendency of these ideas, of
course, not entirely with the stated objectives of the
Commission. Yet it is the tendency which is most important when we are thinking in terms of developing a
society. Even a jet plane goes from one port to another
inch by inch, as it were. The tendency is toward a to-

talitarian society, however far we may be from that destination. We should attend more closely to those who have lived in such a society, and listen to what they protest against. Czeslaw Milosz was not bemoaning the shortage of shoes or the long hours of work under communism when he wrote the following:

> When . . . I stand before Zeus (whether I die naturally, or under sentence of History) I will repeat all this that I have written as my defense. Many people spend their entire lives collecting stamps or old coins, or growing tulips. I am sure that Zeus will be merciful toward people who have given themselves entirely to these hobbies, even though they are only amusing and pointless diversions. I shall say to him: "It is not my fault that you made me a poet. . . . I felt that if I did not use that gift my poetry would be tasteless to me and fame detestable. Forgive me." And perhaps Zeus, who does not call stamp-collectors and tulipgrowers silly, will forgive.[14]

Ominous Implications

Mr. Milosz has seen that there can be no room for the human spirit in a society animated by necessity (called History in the communist orbit), in a planned society, in a society where all activities must be socially significant, where the common good is the final arbiter of what can be done.

The tendency of the ideas of the proponents of the half-way house, as exemplified by the Report of the Commission, is ominous. They imply that there are no

---

[14] Czeslaw Milosz, *The Captive Mind* (New York: Vintage, 1955), p. 240.

hard choices confronting us, that we can have both free enterprise and government guaranteed security, that we can increase collective action with little danger to individual liberty, that the federal government can be extended into virtually every area of life without deadening initiative. But choice is the *sine qua non* of freedom just as it is the heavy price of freedom. The individual cannot participate in a group without yielding up some of his autonomy to the group. He cannot accept aid from others without having his existence conditioned by that aid. It is unlikely that there will be government aid without government control, *nor should there be*. It is the height of irresponsibility to spend public tax money without control over how it is to be spent.

If words were facts, if to say so made a thing so, the half-way house would be a substantial structure. There should be no doubt that vagueness of language and looseness of thought has been used to create a verbal illusion of compatibility between individualism and collectivism. If words would do the job, we could maintain our traditional values—individual liberty, personal independence, and private realms—by the adoption of a social ethic which leaves no room for them. Of course, the half-way house is a mirage, conjured up along with a make-believe universe where such things are possible.

The real world is the one in which Socrates drank the cup of hemlock, in which Jesus of Nazareth was crucified, in which Columbus died in disgrace. It is a world of hard and unpleasant choices, in which the right choices sometimes lead to apparent defeat, in which the nation unwilling to risk failure by maintaining its principles *will* fail because it will be corrupted by its own actions. It is one in which the man who fears to stand on his own two feet may find help to stand, but he will be propelled in undesired or unchosen directions by those who uphold him. It is a world in which you can't have your cake and eat it, too.

The Source of Rights

Take another matter. Is the notion that rights are granted by governments in keeping with the American tradition? More broadly, is the new collectivist ideology in keeping with the American tradition?

To lay claim to certain rights is in keeping with American tradition. To hold that some rights should be inviolable has precedents antedating the Declaration of Independence, for the Rights of Englishmen were recognized in colonial charters of the seventeenth century. Thus, there has never been a time in the history of English America when the inhabitants did not believe that they were entitled to some rights. Further, from colonial times to the mid-twentieth century the insistence upon certain rights has been a central theme in our history. Our attention, however, must be focused upon what rights were claimed, and what changes have occurred.

The earliest grants of rights to Americans stemmed from the King of England. His authority derived from his claim to rule by Divine Right. But in the course of the seventeenth century a momentous change occurred in men's beliefs about the source of their rights. Thinkers began to reason that rights derived directly from

Nature whence they had been implanted by God, rather than indirectly by Divinely appointed authority. This view was used by John Locke to justify the Glorious Revolution in England, and by the time of the American Revolution it had been accepted by most thinking Americans. The rights which Americans claimed and instituted protections of in our revolutionary era were referred to as Natural Rights.

The Natural Rights Doctrine can be succinctly summarized. It held that God had created the universe and that in so doing, as Alexander Hamilton put it, "the Deity . . . has constituted an eternal and immutable law, which is indispensably obligatory upon all mankind, prior to any human institution whatever. This is what is called the law of nature. . . ." After quoting briefly from Blackstone, Hamilton continues his explanation:

> Upon this law depend the natural rights of mankind: the Supreme Being gave existence to man, together with the means of preserving and beautifying that existence. He endowed him with rational faculties, by the help of which to discern and pursue such things as were consistent with his duty and interest; and invested him with an inviolable right to personal liberty and personal safety.
>
> Hence, in a state of nature, no man had any *moral* power to deprive another of his life, limbs, property, or liberty; nor the least authority to command or exact from him, except that which arose from the ties of consanguinity.[15]

---

[15] Richard B. Morris, ed., *Alexander Hamilton and the Founding of the Nation* (New York: Dial, 1957), p. 9.

These, then, were the foundations upon which Americans based their rights when they set up the institutions of civil society in the Republic. They were founded upon the reality of a created universe whose Creator had invested with natural laws. The Founders believed that they had used reason to discover these laws, and that they were reasonable. The principles of natural rights, however, need to be more specifically stated. Natural rights were those rights which man would have if there were no governments or other human institutions. They would be rights because no man would have a *right* to take them away, though he might wrongly do so by the use of force. Thus, no man can claim a *right* to the *life* of another. No one has a *right* to the *liberties* of another. In like manner, no man has a *right* to the *fruits of the labor* of another. In short, by nature a man would have the *right* to the *exercise of his faculties in pursuit of his own well-being,* so long as he *did not trespass* upon the equal rights of others.

In a state of nature, however, natural rights would be endangered by the strong, the predatory, and evil combinations of men. Thus civil societies and governments were necessary to prevent the trespass of one man or a group upon the rights of another. In society, according to eighteenth century thinkers, natural rights gave way to civil rights. But this change did not alter the content of liberties; it merely gave social support to them. As Hamilton said: *"Civil liberty is only natural liberty, modified and secured by the sanctions of civil society.* It is not a thing, in its own nature, precarious and dependent on human will and caprice, but it is conformable to the constitution of man, as well as necessary to the well-being of society."[16] It should be clear from this that governments might institute protections of civil rights but that the rights would not stem from governments.

Many Americans feared that the government created to protect the individual in his rights would usurp them itself. As Thomas Jefferson said, "There are rights which it is useless to surrender to the government and which governments have yet always been found to invade. These are the rights of thinking and publishing our thoughts by speaking or writing; the right of free commerce; the right of personal freedom."[17] Jefferson was expressing his discontent with the original United States Constitution because it did not specifically prohibit the government from trespassing upon the rights of the individual.

It was to answer this objection that the first Ten Amendments were added to the Constitution. These amendments were carefully worded. They do not imply a grant of rights by the government; the belief that they do is one of the distortions that has crept into our thought, or been implanted via the positive government concept. They are, instead, limitations upon the government itself. Their phraseology makes this clear: "Congress shall make no law respecting an establishment of religion" (Article I); "the right of the people to keep

---

[16] Morris, *op. cit.*, p. 13.

[17] Edward Dumbauld, ed., *The Political Writings of Thomas Jefferson* (New York: Liberal Arts Press, 1955), p. 57.

and bear Arms shall not be infringed" (Article II); "the right of the people to be secure in their persons . . . shall not be violated" (Article III). The Bill of Rights should be correctly construed as prohibiting the government from trespassing upon natural rights as civil rights.

The New Concept of Rights

The above are the facts, reasons, and principles upon which the rights claimed by our ancestors were based. Now let us examine some of the recently claimed rights to see if we can determine their character. Does every child have a *right* to an education? If so, it must mean that he has a claim upon someone to educate him; for a right to be viable it must be realizable. Education requires a teacher. A teacher must come forth willingly or one must be procured by inducements or coercion. In practice, the problem is one of employing teachers and paying them for their services. The money for payment must be willingly given, or it must be extracted from those who have it by force or threat of force. In either case, however, for a child to have a right to education means that he has a right to the *fruits of the labor* of others. In short, the right to an education can only be established at the expense of another and prior right.

Does everyone have a *right* to an adequate wage? If so, it must mean that he has a claim upon someone to pay it to him. Suppose that the workman does shoddy work, that he does not produce goods in sufficient amount to reward his employer for a decent wage, that he is incompetent, or that his skills are no longer salable. Does he still have a right to a decent wage?

If he does, it will have to be taken from the *fruits of the labor* of others. The same thing can be said of the right of the farmer to "sell his products at a return which will give him and his family a decent living"; the right of every family to a decent home; the right to adequate medical care, and so forth. The establishment of such rights would be the instituting of perpetual coercion and injustice. Even if enough people would willingly give from the fruits of their labor to provide these benefits, that would not establish them as rights, for no claim to a gift can be established without changing it from a gift to a tax.

Human Rights

Those who favor instituting "economic rights" have invented a supposed distinction between "human rights" and "property rights." These human rights are said to be prior to and superior to property rights. Thinkers who make this distinction are accustomed to refer to all concern with money, finances, and property as selfish and motivated by the desire for "pecuniary" gain, the latter being ignoble and inhuman in its consequences. But property (or monetary) rights are reducible to the rights of human beings to the fruits of their labor and the enjoyment of their life. The expropriation of property or money is an expropriation of that part of the life of a man which he has spent in acquiring or improving his property and earning his money. More, it is an *ex post facto* incursion upon the liberties of the

individual, for it is the taking from a man the product
of his use of his liberty. If the right to the disposal of
his property is not a human right, there are no human
rights.

Enough has been said to enable us to characterize the
nature of most of these latter-day claims to rights. They
must be *provided* by someone or some agency. They are
not founded in the nature of the universe, the nature
of existence, or natural law. Thus, they are arbitrary
creations, the product of the undisciplined imaginations
of men. Can rights be arbitrarily created? If they can,
what would be the effect of doing so? Undoubtedly, language can be used, or abused, to announce an almost
limitless number of rights. Legislatures can embody
such claims in acts, and politicians can run for office
on the basis of them. But what cannot be done is to
make a *grant* of something substantial without removing it from someone who is in possession of it. No one
can be given the right to associate with me without
taking from me my right to choose with whom I will
associate. No one can be given the right to goods which
I produce without taking from me my right to the fruits
of my labor. No one can have a right to my services
without infringing my liberty of serving whom I will.

An arbitrary "right," then, is based upon appearances
rather than reality, upon expediency rather than reason,
upon confusion rather than principles. It is founded
upon the false premise (the appearance) that governments can create rights, that necessity or desirability
can give rise to a just claim, and that a man's life and
liberty can be separated from the fruits of them. An
arbitrary "right" is one which would entail a limitation

on other rights in its normal exercise. A natural right is one which *can be* exercised without trespassing upon the rights of others. It is founded in the nature of human existence. An arbitrary "right" has to be provided; a natural right has only to be acknowledged and protected. Arbitrary "rights" require positive enactment by governments; natural rights require only negative prohibitions.

Rejection of Reality

The natural rights doctrine has been "discredited" in fashionable intellectual circles. This was accomplished by imputing to natural rights philosophers a false conception of the history of man. The defamers of natural rights profess to think that our ancestors believed that man existed at one time in a state of nature, and that the validity of their concepts depends upon the historical existence of such a state. This is not now and never was a valid issue; whether man ever actually existed in a state of nature is wholly irrelevant. Natural rights philosophers based their doctrines upon the nature of reality, not upon the course of historical development. They reasoned that governments were human creations, and that human creations were artificial. By a state of nature they meant the natural condition of man without such human artifices. They were peering beneath the surface of appearances to the underlying reality. They were holding that there is a limiting and lawful reality prior to man-made laws and institutions. This conception of reality has no more been discredited than has the law of gravity.

In order actually to discredit the natural rights doctrine, it will be necessary for thinkers to demonstrate
that we do not live in a confining reality. Let them undertake flight on our planet without attention to the
laws of aerodynamics. Let them show that they can
bestow goods without taking them from their actual pro-
ducers. Let them create rights which will not impinge
upon earlier rights and do not affront man's sense of
justice. Let them submit their Economic Bill of Rights
phrased in the legal language which would permit their
embodiment into law as Constitutional Amendments,
and let us judge whether or not they would result in an
abrogation of the original Bill of Rights.

Natural rights and arbitrary rights cannot exist side
by side in the same society; they are mutually exclusive.
Every effort to create new rights in the twentieth century has already resulted in a diminution of natural
rights as understood in the eighteenth century. There is
an inverse ratio between the right of Americans to the
fruit of their labor and the right of all Americans to a
decent home. The truth of this statement is spelled out
on the deduction side of Everyman's pay check.

Most serious of all is the fact that if government can
create rights, it can withhold and destroy rights. The
practical consequence of this fact is that if rights are
derived from governments, there are no rights. Governmental favors may masquerade as rights. They may
even assume a semblance of constitutionality. But such
favors are instruments of power; they are arbitrary
"rights" granted under the circumstances, subject to
recall and change. When rights are arbitrarily created,
there are no rights, only privileges. The extent to which

we have accepted the belief that children have a right to education, that farmers have a right to a parity of income, that all have a right to the latest medicine, and so on, is the measure of the extent to which we have yielded up our natural rights. It is the degree to which we have sold our heritage for a mess of pottage.

In short, there is no half-way house. Even the illusion of one is builded upon mental images of the shifting sands of expediency. It is rather a direction whose end should begin to emerge from the above analysis. The end is arbitrary government, total and unlimited power in the hands of men (and who watching the machinations of the Kennedy administration can doubt that we are nearer to the end than we had feared), collectivized social existence, and a socialized economy. The occupants of this house, or the creators and participants in an illusion, are impelled by their assumptions toward this end, wittingly or not.

11.

A Rebirth of Liberty

BUT SURELY, I will be told, even
if a rebirth of liberty were needed, now is not the time
for it. What we need in these times, says the critic, are
unity and strength. Surely, it is unwise to cast doubts
upon the benevolence of our government and to divide
our people by calling for a return to liberty. Besides,
times have changed, and we must adjust to and go forward with them. The trend everywhere today is toward
socialism and collectivism, and Americans must adapt
to the actual world within which they live. Even if it
were possible to "turn back the clock," what would our
socialistic allies think of the effort? Speak to us not of
individual liberty but of collective security, for the latter
is what our age requires. Let us shed a tear for the passing of individualism and merge ourselves once more
with the spirit of the times and join in the collective
effort.

Can there be an effective reply to this propagated
"wisdom" of our era? Is it possible to restore liberty, to
return to the path from which we have wandered? Is
individual liberty practical in these complex and dis-
ordered times? If these questions could be answered
affirmatively, would it be possible to arouse people from
their apathy and unconcern with liberty?

But when, let us ask, were the times right for liberty? Surely, no one will say that they were right in 1776. Read again Thomas Paine's description of the world situation in that year: "Every spot of the Old World is overrun with oppression. Freedom has been hunted round the globe. Asia and Africa have long expelled her. Europe regards her like a stranger, and England has given her warning to depart."

Grant that Paine may have been guilty of exaggeration, for his report was not that of a sober reporter but of a man on fire for liberty and independence. Yet a historian can only modify the judgment and eliminate the exaggeration, not deny its validity entirely. Continental European countries were generally ruled by despots, though some of them were called enlightened. The French Estates General had not met in the memory of any living man. Spain was well on the way of its long day's journey into night. The English monarch, George III, was attempting to reassert the declining authority of the English crown. There was not a major republic anywhere in the world. Were these propitious times for liberty?

Historians, with that particular distortion which they almost invariably bring to the past, have, of course, presented a rather different picture of the eighteenth century. They see that people were being sensitized and made ready for liberty by the Enlightenment, by the works of philosophers and scholars, by the thrust of merchants for economic freedom, and by a rising tide of discontent. Yet even as late as 1760 there was no discernible rising tide of discontent even in America. Nor were there many signs of greater political sensitiv-

ity. Voting records for the mid-eighteenth century indicate that even among those who could vote in elections
only a minority did.

Individuals, Ideas, Institutions

We read now of the works of John Locke, Voltaire,
Adam Smith, Montesquieu, and Jean Jacques Rousseau.
But suppose events and developments had taken a different course? It is likely the memory of some of these
men would not have survived their day. Thomas Paine
might have been only a "misguided" polemicist, had
things turned out differently. Who are the great econo-
mists of our day? Shall we remember John Maynard
Keynes and John Kenneth Galbraith? Or will historians
fasten one day on the seminal work of Ludwig von Mises
and F. A. Hayek? The libertarian movement which today appears virtually insignificant may one day be stud-
ied by historians as a sign of a rising tide of freedom.
Stranger things than this have happened in the past.

I do not predict what will happen in the future. Nor
will I accept the predictions of others as to what will be.
So far as I know, the future is undetermined. I do know
with certainty that at one time in the past America
ceased adjusting to the world of its time. Americans did
not follow the trend of Europe but led it. And the example of Americans breaking with the leadership of
Europe and striking out on their own encouraged and
emboldened other men who longed for freedom. How
daring it was in 1776 to throw off monarchy, in 1787 to
conceive a Constitution for which there was no model,
and to rest the government finally upon the consent of

the governed! Was it the times that wrought these things? Or was it Patrick Henry, Thomas Jefferson, Samuel Adams, John Adams, Richard Henry Lee, George Washington, Benjamin Franklin, and those others who struck a responsive chord in the hearts of Americans and guided that response toward the achievement of liberty and independence? I incline to the latter view myself.

But if Americans are unconcerned and apathetic today, leaders would be of no avail, even were they to speak out. It may be, as the critics say, that there is among us little enthusiasm for public undertakings. This may, however, be a hopeful rather than a discouraging sign for liberty. It may mean nothing more than that men are unenthusiastic about welfare programs, that they have tired of a never-ending expediency, that they are weary of vulgar appeals to self-interest narrowly conceived.

Man does not live by bread alone, and materialistic politicians and leaders may be subsisting today on the dregs of appeals which have lost their evocative power. The man with a two-car garage may endure grudgingly yet another proposal to extend social security but be ready and eager to stand for something which will ennoble him and restore meaning to his life. Letters-to-the-editor suggest that there may be millions of Americans who have not yet forfeited the faith of their fathers, who remember still the meaning of liberty and long to see it restored and revitalized.

Could it be that it is the intellectuals and politicians who are out of step? It is possible that words like Liberty, Truth, and Justice might awaken a glad response, had we men with the courage to use them and the sturdiness to exemplify them. Apathy may well be the end product of a stultifying welfare state.

Is it possible to get off the road to collectivism and return to the path of liberty? I think so. As I said in chapter 2, we must retrace our steps if we are to restore liberty in America. This is the least difficult of changes of direction to take. It is the way of rededication, not revolution; of restoration, not innovation; of a return to the tried and true, not an embarking into the unknown.

Superficially, the return to liberty should be easy for Americans. The United States Constitution—the bulwark of our liberty—still provides the higher law in this Republic. Technically it does, anyhow. There have been some regrettable amendments to it, notably the Fourteenth and Sixteenth, and numerous dubious court decisions. But the restoration of liberty can be made within the constitutional framework and would involve to considerable extent a return to that document.

Then, too, there is a great tradition of liberty, for which America was once known round the world. That tradition embraces such concepts as constitutional government, government by law rather than by men, representative government, separation of powers within the government, limited government, and certain inalienable rights belonging to man. These are concepts and principles that can serve as mighty levers for the protection and extension of liberty.

But concepts, institutions, and documents are of little use if men have lost faith in liberty. It is useless to talk of a return to the Constitution if that return is not preceded and accompanied by a vital faith. Faith is essential to all human undertakings for the following reasons: (1) Human knowledge is always limited, partial, and subjected to distorted interpretations resulting from human frailty. (2) Such knowledge as we attain can only be had by a faith that we can obtain it. (3) Faith must precede the works by which we test the validity of our hypotheses. (4) Insofar as we would know of ultimate ends and results, our knowledge is based entirely upon faith.

Faith alone can restore the meaning and urgency to liberty that would cause it to blossom once more in America. Why does liberty matter anyhow? Can it be pragmatically—that is, in terms of its immediate results—justified? There are those who argue that liberty produces material and social benefits, and they appeal to reason and history to support their point of view. But there are others—probably more numerous—who point up the inequalities that result from liberty, who emphasize the unhappiness and warped lives that result from deprivation, who declare that production—which they concede might be advanced by liberty—is no longer the problem. Liberty, they say, is of no account to men who are hungry. The liberty of some must be reduced so that the happiness of all may be advanced. The pragmatic defenders of liberty say this is not so, and retire behind a barrage of statistics to prove their contention. But alas, there are statistics and statistics, and the lesson of history is neither so plain nor human vision so clear that any one answer must be accepted.

Even if the pragmatic defenders of liberty were right, and liberty will provide the most goods with the most equitable distribution in the long run, they would be answered by a Harry Hopkins that men do not eat in the long run. More, it is doubtful that the materialistic argument can give that urgency to liberty that can foster its restoration. Today we may be eating the remains of the goose that laid the golden egg, but so long as we are well-fed, not many of us will be concerned to notice it or have the vision to comprehend its meaning.

Liberty and Morality

But there is a higher, nobler, and more forceful justification for liberty, before which materialistic explanations pale. It is simply this: *man is a moral being*. His existence has ethical and spiritual dimensions which give it ultimate meaning. The moral character of his life is evinced in the making of choices. Liberty is that condition within which choices can be made and spiritual growth take place. The greater the degree of liberty the larger the latitude for choice and growth. To put it negatively, when liberty is reduced and taken away, the moral character of human action is limited and the opportunities for growth are diminished.

Within this framework, social planning becomes not simply a debatable method of achieving the production and distribution of goods but rather a diabolical assault upon the meaning and significance of human existence. For social planning reduces the area of *individual* decision and choice. This is so whether the planning is done by a dictator or democratically by a vote of the whole people. The actions of societies and governments have moral consequences, but neither societies nor governments are moral in any significant sense. The ultimate significance of human morality lies in an eternal realm to which no entrance has been promised societies and governments.

There are those who agree that man is a moral being, but who maintain that this is the very justification of their social programs. They want to free man from those economic urgencies which stunt his character and absorb his life.

In order to do this, they take away from all men those liberties by which they produce and distribute goods and relieve men of much of their responsibility for providing for themselves. They introduce a vast immorality into human relations—by taking from those who produce and giving to those who do not—and wonder at the rise of juvenile delinquency, the spread of crime, and the blight of corruption in government. They remove some of the main props of the family and describe the disintegration of the family as a transition.

When men are still not entirely good, they proceed to make them good by legislation. They enact compulsory attendance laws for school children, make plans for teaching morality in the schools, lobby for prohibitions upon the sale of firearms, alcoholic beverages, certain kinds of literature, and gasp in horror at the "intolerance" which they have bred.

Once set upon this road of making man good by law, they apparently will find no place to turn back until they have removed all opportunities to do evil. But in this, too, they are frustrated at every step. For the agencies they invent to control man for good fall into the hands of those who use them for selfish and evil ends.

All of this could have been, and no doubt was, pre-
dicted in advance. Man was so created that he cannot
be *made good*. Goodness, as men know it, is an option
of man. It depends upon free choice and voluntary com-
mitment. He needs all the choices and responsibilities
that can befall him to remain sensitive to the problem
and practiced in the right response. Remove the responsibilities that are by rights those of a man and you take
away the most immediate incentives for right choice.
There is visible evidence of the truth of these remarks,
but their full meaning must be approached from a deep
faith.

Those who have such a faith are ready to learn the
other steps to be taken for a rebirth of liberty. From
this vantage point we can restore the foundations of
American liberty. "The three basic foundations of our
liberty are," as I said, "(1) beliefs which support it, (2)
institutions which protect it, and (3) personal independence without which it is meaningless and impossible." The fundamental beliefs of the founders of American liberty were, as I pointed out in chapter 2: belief
in "natural law, freedom of the mind and will, individual responsibility, and rationalism. These in turn were
given evocative power by the belief that there is a God
who imbedded his immutable laws in the visible universe, that the individual has a worth not measurable
in human terms, that each individual's good is inseparable from the general welfare, and that liberty is
priceless for the individual and socially beneficial."

Are these still viable beliefs? Or have they now been
discredited by scientific and psychological findings? I
have shown how the belief in reason was undermined

by an emphasis upon irrational motives, how freedom
of the mind and will were undercut by deterministic
theories, how individual responsibility was left stranded
when freedom no longer seemed possible, and how new
ideas were brought forward to replace the old by men
with a collectivistic bent.

Appeal to Reason

But was there anything new in all these ideas except
the "scientific" trappings within which they were purveyed? Surely it is no recent discovery that man is a
creature of passions. What philosopher, ancient or modern, has not noted and remarked upon it? Were not the
great Greek philosophers all too conscious of the tendency of man to yield to unreason? For what did saints
and monks go aside from the world and mortify the
flesh if it was not to subdue these unruly passions? Nor
is it a new notion that all material existence is con-
tingent and dependent. Even the belief that all things
are in a state of continual change was advanced by one
of the earliest of philosophers. The great achievements
of thought have been not the recognition of the obviously changing but of the subtly enduring; not the
portraying of the patently ephemeral but the distinguishing of the eternal amidst the flux; not the discovery of
relationship and contingency but the perception of ultimate freedom; not the describing of the tendency of
man to yield to passions but the working out of reason
by which he might overcome them.

The case for reason is not based upon the belief that
man is always reasonable but upon the view that he is

capable of using reason. The claim for requiring reason
in polite discourse is not that it is the sole or even the
most important motive in human behavior but that
reason alone can be profitably dealt with in discourse.
Indeed, reason is not a motive at all but a method. Irra-
tionalists have made much of reason as a motive—in
order to discredit it—but they simply set up a straw
man when they do so. When men have to cast their
selfish aims in the language of reason, they put the best
possible face upon them and have to leave them at the
mercy of rational analysis. If they will not stand up in
discourse, they should and possibly will be discarded.
That men are capable of reasoning and submitting to
the best reason is the only real justification of political
discourse and debate. This is as true today as it was
2,000 years ago.

Man May Earn Freedom

The case for liberty does not hinge upon man's actual
freedom at any given time. Rousseau was drastically
wrong: man is not born free. He is from the moment of
conception dependent upon someone else for sustenance,
and there is reason to believe that as the infant ages,
it becomes more emotionally dependent. We are all
subjected to inner passions and outer influences and
pressures. No, man is not born free, but perchance he
may become progressively free. It is for this end that
liberty is important. A man may, by exercising choice
and initiative, become relatively independent of others
for his livelihood. By so doing, it was once believed and
may still be true, he can become practiced in those ways

that make for moral and spiritual independence. (But let us not claim too much for man. The religious heritage of Christians proclaims that ultimate freedom as a spiritual condition depends upon the Grace of God. The increasing dependency and pervasiveness of doctrines of social dependency gives weight to this position in our day in which men are not noted for piety.) At any rate, it is only by the exercise of choice that man expresses his freedom.

It was not the newness nor even their apparently scientific character that gave such impetus to doctrines of determinism and irrationalism. It was rather the context within which they came. Romantics had taught that nature was good. If this be accepted as a universal, then everything that can be shown to subsist in nature should be accepted as good. Thus, if man was irrational by nature, if he was dependent by nature, then these should be accepted and yielded to. This position introduced a confusion into thought from which we have not yet recovered. It is also a vast simplification of man, the universe, and its meaning.

Here is not the place, however, to disentangle all the knotty issues about nature which have been introduced in the last two centuries. Suffice it to say that the belief in natural law and natural rights can be held without believing that nature is good in human terms. A child can fall to its death from a cliff through the operations of the law of gravity. As such, there is no moral issue involved in this: it is neither good nor bad, though it may be almost unbearably sad to those who have lost the child. Morality enters the picture when willed human action does. If someone pushed the child from the

cliff, then he was the doer of the evil action, not the law
of gravity.

Obedience to natural law is one thing; yielding to natural impulses is another. The first is expedient and
wise; the second may be neither. Neither natural law
nor natural rights are the cause of our morality. They
are conditions within which morality occurs. Once we
have committed an act, natural law may extend it to an
end which we did not foresee or will. It is in this sense
that natural law is thought to reflect the will of God.
Here, too, it is that the attempt to go contrary to natural
(divine) law is punished and brought to naught. It is
within such a framework that natural rights can have
meaning and the belief in them defended.

Political Considerations

But why use so much space writing of theoretical
matters? Why not speak rather of practical matters?
After all, liberty is a practical consideration. Faith and
beliefs are practical matters also. Try to restore liberty
in America without faith and belief and you will have
revolution rather than government by law. Try to convince a man who lacks faith in liberty that we should
revoke the privileged status of organized labor, remove
the acreage allotments and price supports from agriculture, dismiss the boards and commissions which hold so
much arbitrary power over business activity, and repeal
the vast accretions of social legislation. He might agree
with you that liberty would be desirable, but he would
be appalled by the vision of sweated labor, crop sur-
pluses and declining farm prices, concentrated wealth

in the hands of the few, "cutthroat" competition, millions unemployed, hungry, ill-fed, ill-clothed, and with inadequate medical care. Will liberty work? It might, but the risks are too great to try it.

My point is that we can only persuade men to return to liberty when we can persuade them that there is something at issue worth suffering and dying for, that there are ultimate issues involved. Supported by such a faith, men can recapture the faith and regain the experience that liberty will work. But it will work only to the extent that men are devoted to making it work. That worker will be paid low wages who does not exert himself to attract a higher offer. Those men who band together in a union and strike will find themselves without jobs if they cannot convince the employer that he stands to lose more by giving up their experience than he will gain by the lower wages of those he employs. The farmer will find his income diminished with the loss of price supports if he does not turn to the production of scarce crops that will net him a better return.

But circumstances have changed since the eighteenth century, the defender of the status quo will say, and the liberty that was appropriate to those times is no longer practical. Circumstances have changed, indeed. I have been at some pains to point them out. We live in a country that becomes increasingly urbanized and industrialized. Independence is much more difficult to achieve and maintain today than it was in 1800. The economy is much more intricately interrelated, and the inhabitants of the land more interdependent. The mass media play upon us with advertising and propaganda. Worldwide problems beset us.

But are these arguments against liberty? They might rather be powerful arguments for liberty. Complexities require more knowledge and better understanding for operating within them, not arbitrary protections from them. To protect a man from the consequences of living in his society is to support him in his ignorance and ineffectiveness. When circumstances change, those who are devoted to liberty will think of new ways to protect it and defend it, not arguments for reducing it. Radio and television are regulated because the minds of men were bent toward regulation. Libertarians would try to think, instead, of ways of freeing these inventions from control and the privileges that pertain to those who have franchises. The difficulties and problems of our time cry out for free and responsible men to deal with them. Men who are protected will become less effective in their thinking and more feeble in their efforts.

The call for a return to liberty should be cast in positive and hopeful terms, too. Free men are vital and alive. Competition is an invigorating and enlivening thing. Apathy receives its due punishment just as effort is likely to receive its just reward when liberty prevails. Liberty dignifies those who support it because it is a noble cause. Americans should reject the way that leads to a pale imitation of the stultifying socialisms which beset and inactivate European countries. They should embrace the only national purpose that was ever defined for America and work for a rebirth of liberty.

12. (EPILOGUE)

You Can't Turn Back the Clock

PLATFORMS OR programs which acknowledge an indebtedness to the ideals, principles, or social structures and experiences of the past are likely to evoke the protest: "You can't turn back the clock!" The "conservative" supporters of such policies are declared impractical.

Charles Rolo, in a recent review in *Atlantic,* refers to "brainless reactionaries who pine, fruitlessly, for a return to old-fashioned, laissez-faire capitalism." Clinton Rossiter, in a letter to *Time,* denies the rubric Conservative to Barry Goldwater because of his "refusal to accept social and economic changes that have been firmly established in the American way of life, his announced intention of rolling back the course of history to (at the very latest) 1930. . . ."

Is it fact or myth that the past is of no value in judging the soundness of present ideas and programs?

Naturally, if a person is unaware that his own beliefs are of mythological character, he will think that propositions derived from his beliefs are facts. Those who declare that you cannot restore conditions or revive ideas from the past are doing just that.

They assume that history (the past) proves the fu-

tility of looking back—that successful changes result
from acceptance of, and adjustment to, existing conditions. But does the historical record itself warrant such
assumptions? Did Charlemagne accept the existing
chaos and disorder in Western Europe and make the
necessary adjustments to it, or did he attempt to restore
order and security by looking back to the model of
Rome? Did the Italian Renaissance result from an acceptance of a then decadent medieval culture, or was it
spurred by an attempt to reincarnate the best of Greece
and Rome? Does Mozart's thrilling music indicate a
simple adjustment to Newton's "New Cosmology," or
were both Newton's ideas and Mozart's music informed
by the classical ideas of order, proportion, harmony, and
regularity? There is no adequate way to answer these
questions without exposing the flimsy and unsubstantial
historical basis for the belief that looking backward has
no value.

Evolution Creates a Myth

The view that the past cannot be recovered with
profit rests upon the most extensive myth created in the
modern era. The origin of most myths is obscure; not
so this one. It came into being in an era when men
prided themselves upon their enlightened awareness of
their assumptions. As a myth, the view that a return to
the past is retrogressive can be traced directly to the
evolutionary theories stemming from Darwinism. Dealing with the myth simply as an idea, it is the idea of
progress. The idea of progress, however, was not so
heavily freighted with assumptions before its infusion

with Darwinism. It came to the fore in the seventeenth and eighteenth centuries and is particularly associated with the intellectual development known as the Enlightenment. At this stage, it consisted mainly of the belief that man was coming to know the world in which he lived and that this new knowledge would enable him to control the world or to live a richer life within it. Thus, the idea of progress was initially the notion that man can come to know his nature, the nature of the universe, and the laws of nature, and to make progress by utilizing this knowledge.

But when this idea of progress was infused with Darwinian concepts, it acquired a whole new cargo of meanings and overtones. It acquired a host of metaphysical assumptions which were implicit in the generalizations propagated by the early evolutionists: namely, that the whole universe is in a constant state of evolution, that everything which exists is a result of an evolution, that all life has evolved and is subject to such laws as may govern evolution, that the basic law governing life is a contest with other life for the means to maintain life, that in the contest the fittest survive and progress takes place. Progress became something which takes place automatically, whether man will or no. By the strange logic of the spread of ideas, the "laws" of evolution were extended to social organizations, institutions, and ideas; they too evolved. The latest was the best by virtue of its existence; it was the fittest because it had survived.

When it had taken on all this cargo, the idea of progress had become a myth. It was universal in its application and comprehensive in its coverage. No matter that it was the creation of intellectuals, it entered into the lore of the people. Evidence was available on every hand to support the myth, just as the myth itself served to move men along lines of development consonant with it. The evidence appeared to indicate that man was the latest in the chain of evolution and obviously the best. Was he not the most complex, the most adaptable, the highest of the animals? Were not the material conditions of mankind improving as evidenced by better roads, swifter means of transportation and communication, greater production and wider distribution of goods? With new developments in medicine, dread diseases were controlled, and the average life span was extended. In the nineteenth century, institutions were "perfected" which protected the liberty of the individual, and histories were written showing the evolution of freedom through the centuries. The latest was obviously the best in that it was faster, safer, more efficient, saved labor, provided more goods, extended freedom, and made life more certain.

As the myth gained adherents, philosophy and reason yielded up their role in human affairs. Change is not the result of conscious thought; it is inevitable, driven by subterranean or cosmic forces: the Unknown of Spencer, the contest for the available goods in which the fittest survive of Darwin, the interplay of heredity and environment of Julian Huxley, the adjustments which attend technological innovations of Marx, the energy made available by the sublimation of sex. As William Graham Sumner said, "The things which will change it [the stream of time or history] are the great discoveries and inventions, the new reactions inside the social organism, and the changes in the earth itself on account of changes in the cosmical forces."

With the intellectuals embracing a view which pronounced them superior to their predecessors, the myth was spared subjection to logical analysis or exposure of its metaphysical assumptions. Why, for example, did each change constitute improvement or progress? By what criterion is a speed of 200 miles per hour preferable to one of 100 miles per hour? By what criterion is machine production superior to skilled hand production? It is possible, of course, to name criteria in terms of which these changes would be progress. But the criteria would not be based upon the evidence but upon assumptions or beliefs as to what is desirable. In other words, the criteria would rest upon the *a priori* and metaphysical assumptions about the purpose of life held by the men who maintained them.

The myth acted also to inhibit certain kinds of historical study. Here is a paradox. Evolution made the study of everything basically historical—the study of its evolution or development. But it also made historical study almost purely academic, as that word is now understood. Any study probing into the past must be dealing with dead fossils, for all that was good still survives since the fittest always survives. Of course, ideas are rarely carried to such an extreme, and they are seldom if ever realized. So, under the impetus of evolution the study of history has flourished. But it is a history with only an academic *raison d'etre*, only for its entertainment value. It is the study of the past upon which the present stands, but it is disjoined by the myth from having much to do with the future. To return to anything in the past would be devolution, if it were even possible.

The above is an outline of the myth: the belief that the latest is the best, that the past is irretrievable, that progress is inevitable, and that you can't turn back the clock. It is my belief that we usually read the historical record through the distorted lens ground to the specifications of the myth. In other words, we see history from the perspective of the myth, and read into it evidence to support the assumptions. The view that man, institutions, societies, and beliefs follow evolutionary patterns is based upon *a priori* assumptions which derive from evidence built up from a study of inanimate objects, plants, and animals. The truth of these assumptions can best be tested by doubting their validity.

Western Traditions

Certainly, Western men prior to the eighteenth century had been much more inclined to look back to the past for guidance and direction than to accept the latest as the best. Most peoples have had their lives founded in the customs and traditions of the past. They have thought of any change as a harbinger of chaos and disintegration. It would be much better to continue with that which had been tested and found workable than to venture into the unknown. When men have had rights and privileges, they have been founded in past grants and ideas. To have been fashioned of old was long believed by men to be an argument in favor of a thing.

Looking backward to the past, attempting to revive something from the past, revering the aged was based on assumptions which had mythological bases frequently, just as does the current rejection of the past. Many peoples have believed in the myth of a Golden Age in the past. This myth may refer to the profound belief in the Fall of Man, the lost harmony with God or with the universe, the great age of the Greek city-states, the *Pax Romana,* or any other past condition.

To Christians, the yearning to restore the past was supported by the desire to restore the lost harmony between God and man. Men in the Middle Ages looked backward to the Incarnation of Christ by which the means for the restoration of harmony was made available. They looked back to the age of the Apostles and the Fathers when the word was fresher and purer, not yet so corrupted by the passage of time. The Protestant reformers, for the most part, wished to return to the purity of primitive Christianity.

I do not intend here to argue that these earlier myths were more nearly true than current ones, though they may have been. My point is that other men have revered the past as profoundly as we reject it. Since they did so, their actions provide historical evidence as to the viability of restoring something from the past. What I would like to do here is simply to rescue historical evidence from the limbo into which it has been cast by the believers in the myth of progress.

The possibility of turning to the past with profit should not be confused with attempts to restore the past *in toto.* It is not necessary to show that the Roman Empire was restored in facsimile in the Middle Ages to demonstrate that the attempt to do so had salutary results. Roman law was not restored in its pristine purity in Western Europe in the twelfth and thirteenth centur-

ies, but its revival brought reason to many judicial proceedings and gave impetus to legal thought. Sir Thomas
More did not divide England into city-states, but he and
his fellow humanists did succeed in making the Greek
language and literature a part of the intellectual equipment of educated Englishmen. Perhaps the Protestant
reformers did not restore primitive Christianity, but in
attempting to do so they did revitalize Christianity and
make it a live and relevant religion for millions for centuries. Who would deny that when thinkers of Medieval
Europe turned backward to Aristotle that intellectual
life received new vigor? The United States was hardly
envisioned as a Roman city-state, but she was styled a
republic, her upper legislative house was called the Senate, and she adopted a constitution in the manner of
Rome. Were all of the above "brainless" efforts to turn
back the clock?

It does not follow, of course, that every attempt to
restore something from the past is commendable or
that all experiments with the new are misguided. I am
attempting to redress an imbalance in emphasis, an
imbalance maintained by the support of a modern
myth. Historically, once we ignore the myth, looking
backward has been a very fruitful pastime. It has been
the source of periodic renascences of the Christian era.
Far from being "brainless," it may be the only sensible
alternative to deterioration and chaos at this time. It is
a commonplace today that we live in an age of transition. An age of transition to what? Here the prophets
become vague and suggest that we cannot know, we
shall just have to wait and see. Is there really any *reason*
to suppose that if we sit passively waiting for what may

come that anything but disintegration will come? To return once more to history purged of the myth of progress, the new has come when men have been caught up in new visions, new enthusiasms, when they have been revived and restored. More often than not, it seems to me, this has been spurred by a return in some way to the past.

Answers May Be Found in the Past

There are numerous questions today that should be referred to the past in the hope of finding answers. For example: Have the liberties of men been protected by concentration of power in governments, or by the limitation upon and separation of power? Has the vitality of a people been enhanced by governmental assistance, or by leaving them on their own to look after their own needs? Does desirable change result from the activities of disciplined men, or is it the result of blind chance? Or let us turn to the past in another way: Have some men in earlier times held nobler ideals than men do today? Have more gracious manners been promulgated prior to those of Amy Vanderbilt? Have more worthy purposes of life been enunciated in earlier times? Is Christianity dead, or does its revival depend upon a new vision of ancient meanings?

I am not suggesting that the answers to these questions are simple or easily discovered. What I am saying is that some of the answers may be found in the past, that these are vital questions, and that there is no reason why we should not turn to the past as one of the sources of solutions. We do have much more reason for

doubting that the latest is the best than did men in the
nineteenth century. The life span has been extended but
the continuation of life itself has been thrown into doubt
by the development of nuclear weapons. The latest political institutions are totalitarian states, hardly refuges
of freedom. Concentration camps, military dictatorships,
juvenile delinquency, and huge military expenditures
are endemic twentieth century developments. The myth
of progress now inhibits thought and action, whatever
its role in earlier times.

The myth will not be easily exorcised. Those under
its sway have a whole arsenal of arguments that I have
not touched. They hold up as spectors past brutalities
and cruelties which would be returned when anything
from the past is restored. But is there evidence that an
attempt to restore any one thing will result in restoring
everything? Authority might be restored to the home
without restoring brutality toward children or women.
Rule by law rather than by men could be restored without returning capital punishment for stealing a pig. It
is true that freedom and responsibility cannot be restored without exposing men to inconveniences and
possible suffering. Vitality cannot be restored to modern
life without reviving an awareness of perilous choices
which confront us each moment. Reason cannot be restored to public deliberations without subordinating human passions and desires to it. Rescuing the living value
of the past will not enable us to build utopia. It will
broaden immensely our experience and widen the range
of our choices, as well as heighten our awareness of the
possibility of choice.

Looking backward can be an exhilarating and rewarding experience. There are whole mental worlds of wisdom available to us once we view man's past achievements, failures, and aspirations creatively. There are live wires, to borrow a phrase from William James, running through the whole course of history. We neglect the values of the past to our impoverishment; we plunge into the future unguided by the past at our peril. With so many riches from our own American past, we ought not to be inhibited from using them by the myth that you can't turn back the clock.

The Concept of
Democracy and John Dewey

ONE OF THE MOST often used words in the current American (and world) vocabulary is *democracy*. It adorns the titles of books and textbooks, is the staple concept of political speeches, provides the ballast for propaganda, is the subject of prayers by ministers, and is the basic assumption of social commentaries and polemics. It is almost invariably used approvingly, serving as the criterion against which events, developments, practices, and institutions are measured. A desirable program of action is called "democratic," one which is opposed is called "undemocratic." There is nothing particularly strange about this usage; it supposedly serves to denote an agreed-upon set of values.

But what are these agreed-upon values? The trouble enters at this point, for democracy is one of the most vague and imprecise words in our vocabulary. It has lost most if not all of its descriptive value. Contrariwise, it has picked up meaning in some kind of inverse proportion to its loss of descriptive accuracy. Democracy, as a word, is full to overflowing with meaning or, more correctly, with meanings. It is so full of meanings that it has the long distance accuracy of a shotgun, as it were, in precise expression. It has become a loaded word.

Before examining the consequences of this development the word needs first to be unpacked of its meanings. Democracy must first be defined so that the basic definition can be set beside the accretions of meanings attached to it.

Democracy was originally an exclusively political concept. The first-listed definitions in recent dictionaries preserve this sense of the word. The *New Twentieth Century Dictionary* (unabridged) gives as the first definition of democracy: "Government by the people; a form of government in which the supreme power is lodged in the hands of the people collectively." The first meaning in the *American College Dictionary* is "Government by the people; a form of government in which the supreme power is vested in the people and exercised by them or by their elected agents under a free electoral system." In essence, both dictionaries have said that democracy primarily refers to a form of government in which the people rule. Etymologically, the word means simply rule by the people, the citizens, or the masses.

Even in the political sense, however, democracy has acquired additional connotations, overtones, and meanings. Textbooks in American government indicate this trend. For example, one recent textbook says that democracy means government by the many, government directed by the popular will, government in the interest of the people, government by the consent of the governed, "belief in the Christian ideal of the unique value

and dignity of individual human beings," in human
equality, and in the possession of certain human freedoms.[1] Another textbook includes, in addition to the
usual meanings overlapping with some of the above,
these two notions: a variety of particular programs, and
limited government.[2]

Some of these meanings are not clearly related to the
basic definition of democracy. For example, why is democratic government limited government? Because the
people govern, it does not follow that they will automatically limit the exercise of power by their government. The limitations on the powers of government in
the American political system were written into the Constitution, and these limits were conceived in the light
of certain natural rights because they were believed to
belong to man, not because they inhered in popular government. Rule by the people may not necessarily be
founded on any "Christian ideal." What these authors
are trying to do, of course, is to tell what democracy in
America means to Americans, and, to some extent how
it is practiced in America. They have confused it with
American practices, adding to it associated meanings,
and some which are not necessarily if at all related to it.

Thus far, democracy has been dealt with as a political
concept. But it is by no means restricted to a political
context in its present usage; it has ramified into all
areas of life. It is true there is some imprecision in its

---

[1] Harold R. Bruce, *American National Government* (rev.
ed.; New York: Holt, 1957), pp. 5-9.

[2] James M. Burns and Jack W. Peltason, *Government by
the People* (Englewood Cliffs, N. J.: Prentice-Hall, 1957,
third edition), pp. 8-13.

use in the political context examined already, but this is
negligible compared to the looseness which characterizes
the general use of it.

There is no better place to discover this profusion of
meanings and connotations attached to democracy than
in the writings of John Dewey. His is the example par
excellence of the extension of the meaning of democracy into every phase and activity of life. It would be
difficult, if not impossible, to find a writer who has used
the word democracy with a greater variety of meanings
or with more imprecision.

For most men to use words imprecisely is not surprising, but for John Dewey to have done so is remarkable.
Dewey was a philosopher, and philosophers have tradi-
tionally defined their key concepts carefully and rigidly,
rigorously following their established definition. Yet
Dewey's practice went directly counter to this. Democracy was one of his key concepts, if not *the* key concept.
He used the word often enough. He wrote at least one
book[3] and numerous articles with democracy in the
titles.[4] In one article he used the words democratic and
democracy twenty-nine times.[5] Yet he concluded the

---

[3] John Dewey, *Democracy and Education* (New York:
Macmillan, 1916).

[4] Some examples in addition to the titles listed in the foot-
notes below are: "Industrial Education and Democracy,"
Survey, XXIX (March 22, 1913); "Practical Democracy,"
New Republic, XLIV (December 2, 1925); "Democracy in
Education," *National Education Association Journal*, XVIII
(December, 1929).

[5] John Dewey, "The Challenge of Democracy to Educa-
tion," *Progressive Education* (1937), reprinted in John Dewey,
Problems of Men (New York: Philosophical Library, 1946).
Page numbers cited are from *Problems of Men.*

article with this observation: "I don't know just what democracy means in detail . . . at the present time. I make this humiliating confession the more readily because I suspect that nobody else knows what it means in full concrete detail."[6] In short, Dewey did not define precisely one of his key concepts.

Nor does the difficulty in understanding the meaning which Dewey attached to words end with democracy; a similar imprecision was characteristic of most of his writing. Joseph W. Beach declared that Dewey's work showed "a lack of clearness, a lack of precision."[7] Among the difficulties in his style, according to another critic, were "the use of familiar words with unfamiliar meanings; the use of words with pregnant meanings; the use of long, involved and highly concentrated sentences . . . ; the development of different important ideas in the same paragraph. . . ."[8]

All of this means that it is frequently impossible to determine the way in which he is using a word by its context. My aim here is to set forth the variety of meanings which Dewey attached to the word democracy, but some of his usages defy classification. For example, he asks the question: "How far is science taught in relation to its social consequences, actual and possible, if the resources which science puts at human disposal were utilized for general democratic social welfare?"[9] Not only is the question indecipherable, but the

[6] *Ibid.*, p. 56.

[7] As quoted by Herman H. Horne, *The Democratic Philosophy of Education* (New York: Macmillan, 1932), p. xii.

[8] *Ibid.*, p. xiii.

[9] Dewey, *Problems of Men,* pp. 52-53.

meaning of "democratic" in this context is not available by analysis. Consequently, I have not attempted to classify this usage.

But without this particular enigmatic usage Dewey used democracy with an astounding array of connotations and associations. While my tally is not definitive, Dewey used the words democracy and democratic in at least thirty ways, either as meanings, connotations, significations, or associations. The meanings overlap, intertwine, and intermingle in an indistinct fashion, but each of them has something which distinguishes it slightly from the other. Let us examine them.

Democracy, according to John Dewey, is:

1. a political system, involving such institutions as "universal suffrage, recurring elections, responsibility of those who are in political power to the voters. . . ."[10]

2. government by the consent of the governed.[11]

3. an educational process.[12]

4. an educational principle.[13]

5. an educational system, one in which all participate in making the decision and all make contributions to the common life.[14]

6. a method, one of reaching decisions by discussion, voting and the acceptance of the majority view.[15]

---

[10] *Ibid.*, pp. 57-58.
[11] *Ibid.*, p. 35.
[12] *Ibid.*, p. 36.
[13] *Ibid.*, p. 34.
[14] *Ibid.*, p. 63.
[15] John Dewey, *Freedom and Culture* (New York: Putnam, 1939), p. 128.

7. constantly changing. As Dewey put it, "The very idea of democracy . . . must be continually explored afresh . . . to meet the changes that are going on in the development of new needs on the part of human beings and new resources for satisfying these needs."[16]

8. concerned with the needs and wants of people, "that asking other people what they would like, what they need, what their ideas are, is an essential part of the democratic idea."[17]

9. a guide for directing the forces which confront man in his daily living.[18]

10. a kind of freedom. Dewey speaks of "democratic freedom,"[19] saying that "it designates a mental attitude rather than external unconstraint of movements. . . ."[20]

11. a criterion for making judgments about conditions, developments, and institutions.[21]

12. a theory of knowledge. Dewey says that democracy "must develop a theory of knowledge which sees in knowledge the method by which one experience is made available in giving direction and meaning to another."[22]

13. closely related to science and the scientific method. He indicates in connection with his call for a demo-

---

[16] Dewey, *Problems of Men*, p. 47.

[17] *Ibid.*, p. 35.

[18] *Ibid.*, p. 48.

[19] Dewey, *Freedom and Culture*, p. 129.

[20] Dewey, *Democracy and Education*, p. 357.

[21] *Ibid.*, pp. 139-40, 376.

[22] *Ibid.*, p. 401.

cratic theory of knowledge that the "recent advances in physiology, biology and the logic of the experimental sciences supply the specific intellectual instrumentalities demanded to work out and formulate such a theory."[23] On another occasion he said: "While it would be absurd to believe it desirable or possible for every one to become a scientist when science is defined from the side of subject matter, the future of democracy is allied with the spread of the scientific attitude."[24] It is not clear whether science is democratic or democracy is scientific, or both.

14. an attitude.[25]

15. a belief in a humanistic culture.[26]

16. an economic system, a system "in which all share in useful service and all enjoy a worthy leisure."[27]

17. a standard for personal conduct.[28]

18. a form of social control. Here the meaning is fairly clear as it refers to political democracy. He means that when an individual participates in the making of decisions he binds himself to follow the decision made, whether it is in accord with his wishes or not.[29]

---

[23] *Ibid.*

[24] Dewey, *Freedom and Culture*, p. 148.

[25] *Ibid.*, p. 125.

[26] *Ibid.*, p. 124.

[27] Dewey, *Democracy and Education*, p. 300.

[28] Dewey, *Freedom and Culture*, p. 130.

[29] Dewey, *Problems of Men*, p. 35.

19. a way of organizing society. Dewey frequently used the phrase, "democratic society,"[30] meaning a society so organized that all may participate in its decisions, its goods, the formulation of its ideas and aims, and to which all may contribute.[31]

20. a belief in equality. Equality is essential to democracy and inextricably tied up with it, Dewey thought. By equality he meant several things as usual. "All individuals are entitled to equality of treatment by law and its administration." He means equality of opportunity also. "The very fact of natural and psychological inequality is all the more reason for establishment by law of equality of opportunity, since otherwise the former becomes a means of oppression of the less gifted."[32] Dewey passed over without comment the probability that government assurance of equality to the less gifted might be an "oppression" of the more gifted. Let there be no doubt about it, the whole tendency of Dewey's thought was leveling, the breaking down of all distinctions which raise one person or thing above another. To indicate the extent of his thinking in this direction, his comment regarding distinctions made in philosophy is revealing. "Democratic abolition of fixed differences between 'higher' and 'lower' still has to make its way in philosophy."[33]

---

[30] For example, see Dewey, *Democracy and Education*, pp. 142, 357, 376.

[31] See also Dewey, *Problems of Men*, pp. 37, 74.

[32] *Ibid.*, p. 60.

[33] *Ibid.*, p. 15.

21. the belief in the dignity and worth of the individual.[34]

22. participation in the "formation of the values that regulate the living of men together. . . ."[35]

23. "primarily a mode of associated living, of conjoint communicated experience."[36]

24. an act of faith from the believer.[37]

25. a set of aims or ends.[38]

26. an ideal, though what he meant was something to be striven for, not an ideal in the Platonic sense.[39]

27. a way of life.[40]

28. a form of life.[41]

29. a living thing, if Dewey's language is to be interpreted literally. For instance, he says that "democracy in order to live must change and move. . . ." "If it is to live" it "must go forward. . . . If it does not go forward, if it tries to stand still, it is already starting on the backward road that leads to extinction."[42]

---

[34] *Ibid.*, pp. 44-45.
[35] *Ibid.*, p. 58.
[36] Dewey, *Democracy and Education*, p. 101.
[37] For example, see Dewey, *Freedom and Culture*, p. 126.
[38] *Ibid.*, pp. 93, 176.
[39] Dewey, *Democracy and Education*, p. v.
[40] Dewey, *Problems of Men*, pp. 57-58.
[41] *Ibid.*, p. 47.
[42] *Ibid.*

242 THE FATEFUL TURN

30. a concept for the organization of every aspect of a society and its culture, including all areas of life in its extended meaning. Dewey said: "The problem of freedom and democratic institutions is tied up with the question of what kind of culture exists. . . ."[43] And, "The struggle for democracy has to be maintained on as many fronts as culture has aspects: political, economic, international, educational, scientific and artistic, religious."[44]

In sum, then, according to Dewey, democracy is a political system, an economic system, a social system, and an educational system. It is a criterion for judgments, a theory of knowledge, a method, a principle, an aim, an ideal, a thing in itself. It is a way of life, a form of life, a form of associated living, a guide for living, a matter of faith. It is equalitarian, humanistic, scientific, concerned with the needs and wants of man, constantly changing and growing. It calls for a particular kind of organization of society and a particular orientation of all aspects of the culture. In short, according to Dewey, democracy applies to all areas and aspects of life. If anything was left out we may be sure that it was an error of the head and not of the heart.

In addition to these multifold descriptive meanings attached to democracy there is the nondescriptive usage alluded to in the beginning—democracy as an agreed-upon value which is to be realized in the society, an unquestioned good. This amounts to a normative usage

[43] Dewey, *Freedom and Culture*, p. 13.
[44] *Ibid.*

without a norm. Reduced to its essentials it amounts to saying that there is something good to be sought, but what the good is cannot be definitely stated.

But if democracy is fraught with all the meanings that John Dewey attaches to it, is it such an unalloyed good? Before deciding whether democracy is good and desirable it is necessary first to know what it is. Otherwise, it is like signing a blank check, to be filled in according to circumstances. To demonstrate this, let us accept temporarily the varied meanings which Dewey says belong to democracy. Let us observe a man before a congressional investigating committee who is being examined on his beliefs.

Suppose the chairman of the committee asks him this question: "Are you a democrat?" How could he answer such a question if he accepts Dewey's meanings? Suppose he says, "Yes, I am a democrat." What is he saying? Does he believe in associated living? If so, what forms of associated living does he believe in? Polygamy? Communism? Complex marriage? Does he believe in a "democratic" economic system? Is it to be equalitarian? Do all share equally in the wealth? Does he believe that the more gifted are to be restricted to a level with the less gifted? Does he think that all should have their needs and wants met equally regardless of ability or effort? Does he believe that all men should share in the formation of values, or does he believe that values exist and men seek them, a perfectly respectable philosophical position? Is he sufficiently scientific to be a democrat, or is he so "backward" as to hold that science does not deal with all of reality?

Before this array of questions he might change his

answer and deny that he was a democrat. But he would
only have changed horns on the dilemma. Does he mean
to deny the worth and dignity of the individual? Does
he reject this "Christian ideal"? Is he opposed to freedom? Is he against government by the consent of the
governed? Does he have the audacity to question the
validity of an idea stated in the Declaration of Independence—that all men are created equal?

It should be apparent that the question raised by the
chairman poses intolerable alternatives. Any witness
confronted with such a question, involving so many possible interpretations of the meaning of a word, would
have every reason for pleading the Fifth Amendment, for
nothing is more likely than that he would "incriminate"
himself if he tried to answer it. With all these hosts of
meanings the word cannot be used with sufficient exact-
ness to ask or to state anything. If a congressional committee found it necessary to get the answer to such a
question, it would be necessary first to issue cards to
"true democrats." Then the committee could ask an
answerable question: "Are you a card-carrying democrat?"

None of this should be interpreted to mean that
Dewey's use of the word democracy was merely ridiculous. Nothing could be further from the truth. Analysis
makes it appear ridiculous, but synthesis presents a different face. Dewey intended to suggest that democracy
was an all-embracing concept, encompassing all areas
and activities of life. He believed that if democracy was
to exist at all, it must be applied in all aspects of the life
of the people. In other words, democracy is an ideology,
a complex of interrelated ideas.

There is not space here to show how all the pieces fit into the whole, but it can be at least suggested. Dewey started with the view that democracy means equal participation by all in making decisions and sharing in the benefits of society. For this to be put into practice numerous conditions must be met. If there are great inequalities in wealth, there will be consequent inequalities in power and the subsequent ability to participate. Therefore, gross inequalities in wealth must be wiped out. The graduated income tax, for example, would be a device for accomplishing this in part.

But, people do not have equal abilities. To give equal opportunity to people of unequal abilities there must be some agency to act on behalf of the less gifted. In the schools, for example, infinite attention may be lavished on the less gifted, bringing them to a level with relatively neglected more gifted pupils. Is it possible, then, that Dewey's uncertainty as to the full meaning of democracy lay in the inability to envisage all the steps necessary to assure the realization of democracy? Who *could* imagine all the steps necessary to the making of all men equal?

Dewey, whether he was aware of it or not, made democracy a *total* concept. The application of his ideas to society would be totalitarianism. Dewey was much concerned to preserve the United States from European varieties of totalitarianism, yet in order to do this he proposed total democracy. Totalitarianism is monolithic, one-directional, unitary, demanding total allegiance to an ideology, or to the state which acts to realize the ideology. Under totalitarianism all aspects of life are brought into accord with this ideology, all disruptive ideas or forces are removed. Is this not what Dewey proposed by the "instrumentation" of democracy?

But it may be objected that Dewey loved freedom, that he was the outstanding proponent of diversity. Supposing this were true, it is reasonable to ask how he proposed to buttress freedom or preserve diversity. Primarily, he placed his hopes in participation by the people in the making of decisions. Now it is clear that participation is of the essence of democracy in its original signification, but the relation of participation to freedom is not so clear. Suppose the majority vote to remove some freedom—say, to have censorship of the press. If everyone in the land had voted upon the matter, it would make it no less a lessening of freedom.

It may be objected that the majority will not act in this way, that their participation insures the preservation and extension of liberty. There is little basis in fact for such an assumption. The Nazi party got a plurality of the votes in the last free election held in Germany before World War II. If reports are to be believed, something like 99 per cent of those qualified in the Soviet Union vote in elections. Nor has the extension of suffrage in the United States since the Civil War resulted in new liberties being added in America. On the contrary, there has been a steady attrition of liberty since that time, though the two things are not necessarily related. Participation by the electorate is hardly a guarantee of the preservation of traditional freedom. Diversity is hardly furthered under present conditions of transportation and communication by participation either.

Of course, those who set up the United States government did not derive liberty from men but from man and his nature. They believed that liberty was a natural right according to natural law, not something bequeathed by government or the majority. It was not the right of government to take these liberties away, nor was it the right of the majority, though they might usurp them, even under the United States Constitution, though every impediment was thrown in the way of the people doing so. While some, like Jefferson, believed that participation of the people would tend to preserve these rights, they would not have equated participation with liberty.

Dewey did not believe in natural law and natural rights. His belief in freedom had no such foundation, if it had any foundation at all. There was no arbiter for Dewey beyond what is and what the people want, no natural laws limiting what the people may do and have, nothing beyond the majority to which to appeal. Hence, he placed no limits upon the power vested in the people and did not believe that there were any. *Total* power would be vested in the people. If they accepted his prescription, they would act to realize a total concept— democracy. No doubt, they would act through the government as well as through other agencies (until these agencies were absorbed into the government) in wielding their power. These are the elements necessary to totalitarianism.

The bones of the creature are now laid bare. On the one hand, democracy is an extremely ambiguous word, loaded with a variety of meanings, vague and imprecise. It carries with it also the implication of approval and value. On the other hand, it has become an ideology for the total organization of society. Such a word cannot be

used when the object is clear thought; it should not be
used to promote programs whose acceptance is urged
because they are "democratic." The latter use is argument in a circle. It goes something like this: democracy
is a good to be sought; this program is democratic; ergo,
this program is good and ought to be adopted. Certainly
democracy is not the same thing as freedom, and there
is no reason for using them as synonyms. Representative or popular government is one thing; liberty or freedom is something else.

There is a way out of this circle. Responsible people
will avoid the use of democracy without first defining it.
Having defined it they will restrict themselves to that
usage. Even this may not be enough, however; it has
been used for propaganda, for persuasion, and as a sub-
stitute for political thought so long that it cannot be
easily divested of its accretions of meanings. Anyone
desiring to engage in logical thinking or in reasonable
examination of issues will be very careful in using the
word.

All of this would not be so important if there were
not so great a need for new political thought, or at least
for rethinking our assumptions and beliefs. How long
has it been since an amendment was added to the Constitution extending traditional liberties? Is this because
liberties are not in danger? No! Developments in advertising, in law enforcement, in directing thought, in
bringing pressure, in fighting wars, in taxation, in communication definitely have brought a circumscription
of liberties. Yet twentieth-century America is a waste-
land so far as political thought is concerned. In part,
at least, this absence of thought can be laid to the fact

that thinkers have been mesmerized by the pleasing sound of the word democracy. They should cease their genuflections before this vague, imprecise, and loaded word. Every one of the meanings which Dewey assigned to democracy needs to be examined on its own merit, not artificially bolstered by a magic word.

Index

Aaron, Daniel, 85n
Action, human
  conservatives and, 163
  mass, 14, 69
  motives, 140
  nonrational, 73
  responsible, 37, 48, 81, 133, 154
Adams, Brooks, 49
Addams, Jane, 106
Agricultural Marketing Act, 157
Agriculture
  Department of, 117
  price supports, 169
  problems of, 156
  production, 59
  relief, 158
  tenant farms, 63
Allen, Frederick L., 97
Amendments to Constitution, 61, 121,
  199
America
  compromise, 148
  conformity, 13
  foundations of liberty, 28-39, 40-54,
    214
  goals, 166
  individualism limited, 20, 151
  literature of, 13, 85, 96
  local self-government, 137
  tradition, 57, 92-106, 137, 175, 196
  turning point in history, 177
  way of life, 95, 152
Arbitrary rights, 202, 204
Associations, 109
Atomic theory, 139

Balfour, Lord Arthur, 46
Banks and banking, 158
Beach, Joseph W., 236
Beard, Charles A., 103, 105
Behavior, 50, 96, 133
Bekhterev, Vladimir M., 50
Bellamy, Edward, 85
Blackstone, Sir William, 197
Brandeis, Louis D., 103
Brooks, Van Wyck, 98
Bruce, Harold R., 234n
Bryan, William Jennings, 53
Buckley, William F., Jr., 175
Bureaucracy, 189
Burns, James M., 234n
Business, 65, 118, 151, 158

Capitalism, 170
Calverton, V. F., 100
Canby, Henry S., 101
Cargill, Oscar, 47
Carnegie, Andrew, 74
Carson, Clarence B., 79n
Cash, Wilbur J., 62n
Cather, Willa, 101
Causation, 141
Centralization, 188
Change, 140, 225
Chase, Stuart, 105, 106
Choice-making, 18, 134, 154, 195, 214
Church. *See* Religion
Circumstances hostile to liberty, 20,
  55-70
Civil rights, 198
Civil War, 59, 60, 246
Clock, turning back the, 221-31
Collectivism
  beliefs in, 71, 82, 183
  causes, 128
  compromise in, 149, 163
  Constitution, U.S., 111
  curvature of the mind, 71-91
  group, 109
  historical shift in, 108
  liberty, attack upon, 71, 128
  relativism, 81
  responsibility and, 169
  road to, 107-27
  transitional movement of, 109
  turning point in, 115
  unions in, 90
  views of man, 130
Commager, Henry S., 49n, 51n, 83n,
  84
Commonism and the individual, 13-27
Communication, 68, 155, 179;
  see also Literature
Communism, 170
Compromise, failure of, 148-62, 163
Conformity, American, 13
Conservatism
  "liberal," 164, 174
  liberty, 56
  reformers, 23
  views of, 163, 166
  weaknesses, 55
Constitution, U.S.
  amendments, 61, 121, 199
  collectives disarmed by, 111
  law, 77, 84
Corporations, 118

251